METTERNICH

Metternich

ANDREW MILNE

UNIVERSITY OF LONDON PRESS LTD

ISBN 0 340 18159 1 Boards
ISBN 0 340 15199 4 Paperback

First published 1975

University of London Press Ltd
St Paul's House, Warwick Lane, London EC4P 4AH

Maps drawn by Crispin Fisher

Printed in Great Britain by
Hazell Watson & Viney Ltd, Aylesbury, Bucks

PREFACE

The English student of Metternich is at a double disadvantage
in that the most impressive biography yet written, Heinrich
Srbik's *Metternich, der Staatsmann und der Mensch* (Munich
1925), is not available in the English language and much of the
material that is in English is out of print and the reader is therefore dependent on the resources of libraries.

Some at least of the works that I have found useful are listed
in the further reading chapter, but I would like to thank here
the authors and publishers of the following books from which I
have been permitted to reproduce copyright material: *Metternich*
by Algernon Cecil, published by Eyre and Spottiswoode; *Three
Studies in European Conservatism* by E. L. Woodward, published
by Cass; *Englishmen and Others* by A. J. P. Taylor, published by
Hamish Hamilton; *The Habsburg Empire* 1790–1918 by C. A.
Macartney, published by Weidenfeld and Nicolson; *The Habsburg
Monarchy* by A. J. P. Taylor, published by Hamish Hamilton; *A
World Restored* by H. A. Kissinger, published by Houghton
Mifflin and *Conservatism Revisited* by P. Viereck, published by
Collier Books.

I am also greatly indebted to the Master and Fellows of
Emmanuel College, Cambridge, whose generosity, both in terms
of hospitality and in the granting of library facilities, has helped
enormously in the preparation of this book.

Finally, my thanks are due to colleagues and pupils at Oundle,
whose comments at various stages have not gone unheeded.

CONTENTS

8

CONTENTS

CONTENTS

CONTENTS

efficiency and conciliation 18. The Change of Emperors: *Emperor Francis's will – Opposition to Metternich* 19. The Vor März: *Administration – The economy – The development of articulate opposition*

PART V THE FORCES OF CHANGE 131

20. Collapse of Solidarity 21. Bohemia: *Economic unrest – Problem of the Czech revival* 22. Hungary: *The Diets – Conflict with Széchenyi – Belated conciliation* 23. Galicia: *The abortive revolt of 1846 – The annexation of Cracow – 1848* 24. Italy: *Metternich's policy of repression – conciliatory aims – Metternich loses control* 25. Germany: *Militant patriotic feeling – The Zollverein* 26. The Fall of Metternich: *Metternich's flight* Principal Events 1848–9

PART VI THE PROBLEM OF INTERPRETATION 169

27. The Historians 28. Metternich: An Evaluation

EPILOGUE THE LAST YEARS 180

FURTHER READING 183

Index 185

MAPS

PART 1
The Emergence of Metternich

[1] THE HABSBURG EMPIRE IN 1809

On balance historians have not warmed to Metternich. This is
hardly to be wondered at, for there is little glamour to a man
who sets himself against historical forces to little or no avail and
whose achievement is to be measured not in terms of victory but
in terms of his ability to delay defeat. And yet, failure is a harsh
and damning word and it is easy to overlook the fact that it
covers a wide area. Certainly Metternich was a failure in the
strictest sense of the word. He failed by his own criteria, in that
he failed to bring to the Habsburg Empire a new dynamic and
he failed to sustain the Powers in cooperative loyalty to conservative principles after 1815, but at the same time the very
duration of his dominance in European affairs was surely in some
real sense a success, for few can have expected such a career of
him when at the age of thirty-six and as a relative outsider he
was appointed Minister of Foreign Affairs in October 1809 by
the Emperor Francis. Nor indeed would many have been prepared to predict with any certainty that the Habsburg Empire
had any future at all in the gloomy circumstances of recent defeats at the hands of Napoleon. Metternich's part in the revival
of Habsburg fortunes and the decline of those of Napoleon was
by no means insignificant.

The reign of the Emperor Francis had been one of persistent
discomfort for the Habsburg dynasty. Succeeding to the throne
in 1792, Francis inherited an empire that had been severely
shaken during the late 1780s when a series of revolts had broken

out against the centralising policies of his uncle, Joseph II. The brief but assertive reign of Leopold II (1790–2) had gone some way towards the restoration of stability but Francis, himself not a commanding personality, had then found himself face to face with the French Revolution which, both in theory and in practice, constituted a new and major threat to the Empire's integrity.

The French Revolution and its impact on the Empire

The ideas unleashed by the Revolution were diametrically opposed to the whole philosophy of Habsburg rule. Not only did the executions of Louis XVI and of Marie-Antoinette, his Habsburg wife, represent the ultimate assault on the idea of the divinity of kingship which was fundamental to Habsburg thinking, but there lay in the idea of the rights of 'peoples' to sovereignty both a challenge to the absolutism that Francis took for granted and also the roots of the nationalist creeds which were subsequently to emerge in fundamental opposition to the Habsburg concept of a multi-national empire. 'Nationalism' as a dynamic force was still too weak to command much of a hearing at the Congress of Vienna in 1815 and so this aspect of the Revolution should not be over-stressed at this stage, but the insidious potential of revolutionary ideas was clear enough to Francis, whose worst fears were given early confirmation when two 'Jacobin' plots were unveiled within the Empire in 1794, one in Vienna itself and the other in Hungary.

Meanwhile the ideological militancy of some of the French revolutionaries had led on to militancy in practice. The opening of the Revolutionary War in 1792 meant the start of a long series of military setbacks for Austria, relatively unimportant to start with, involving as they did the loss of the Austrian Netherlands which had always been something of a mixed blessing, but moving relentlessly through to Italy and the first encounters with Napoleon and then on to the heart of the Empire in the battles of Austerlitz in 1805 and Wagram in 1809, which seemed to signal the end of all Habsburg pretensions to independence.

By 1809 morale was so low that the citizens of Vienna responded to the news of defeat at Wagram not with anguish and remorse but with dancing in the streets and Francis was left to wonder whether the 'national resurgence', which his advisers had assured him would reverse the indignity of Austerlitz, had ever been more than a wistful illusion.

The plight of the Empire was indeed a sorry one, for the sequence of Napoleonic victories brought with them the inevitable series of punitive peace treaties. Austrian influence in Italy, Germany, and the Low Countries was relentlessly reduced to nothing. By the Treaty of Campoformio in October 1797 Austria recognised the French annexation of Belgium, secretly promised support for the French claim to the left bank of the Rhine and ceded Lombardy in return for a share in the newly partitioned Venetian possessions and for the Illyrian provinces of Istria and Dalmatia. This situation was confirmed in the Treaty of Lunéville, February 1801. The real rough handling followed later with the Treaties of Pressburg, December 1805, and Schönbrunn, October 1809. In the former Austria lost her Venetian possessions and also Istria and Dalmatia. Furthermore, she lost territory, notably the Tyrol, to Germany, whose new structure Francis was forced to recognise, thereby accepting the passing of Austrian influence there. And this time the consolation prize was smaller, namely Salzburg. Schönbrunn merely turned the screw tighter, with Salzburg now apportioned to Bavaria, the remainder of the Adriatic coastline lost to the Kingdom of Italy and parts of Galicia meted out to Russia and to the Grand Duchy of Warsaw. Francis must have felt that the Habsburg inheritance was slipping through his fingers like sand (see maps, pp. 14 and 15).

Then, as if all this was not enough, there was the mounting economic strain. Even before the wars with revolutionary France the imperial finances had been under pressure. Joseph II's Turkish war (1788–90) had aggravated an already delicate situation and he had embarked on the dangerous expedient of increasing the amount of paper money in circulation. Worse still, in order to maintain public confidence, he had slipped in a

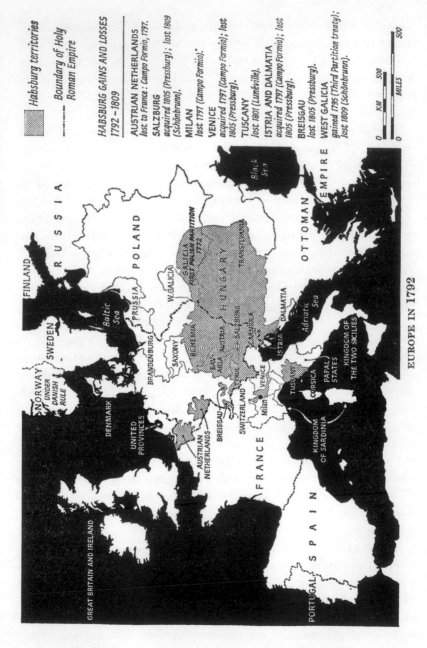

Habsburg territories

— — — *Boundary of Holy Roman Empire*

HABSBURG GAINS AND LOSSES
1792 – 1809

AUSTRIAN NETHERLANDS
lost to France : Campo Formio, 1797.

SALZBURG
acquired 1805 (Pressburg); lost 1809 (Schönbrunn).

MILAN
lost 1797 (Campo Formio).

VENICE
acquired 1797 (Campo Formio); lost 1805 (Pressburg).

TUSCANY
lost 1801 (Lunéville).

ISTRIA AND DALMATIA
acquired 1797 (Campo Formio); lost 1805 (Pressburg).

BREISGAU
lost 1805 (Pressburg).

WEST GALICIA
gained 1795 (Third Partition treaty); lost 1809 (Schönbrunn).

EUROPE IN 1792

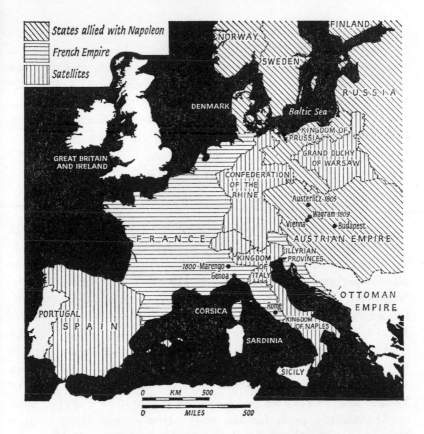

EUROPE AFTER SCHÖNBRUNN 1810

secret issue in 1788 over and above the issues publicly announced. Francis continued to issue more paper, both publicly and secretly, and needless to say the horrors of inflation duly made their appearance. Where there had been roughly twenty-eight million Bankozettel in circulation in 1788 there were slightly over one thousand million in 1811. A violent deflation in that same year, when Count Wallis, the Emperor's latest finance minister, called in all Bankozettel and issued new notes at the rate of one new to five old could not be sustained either and the whole economic trauma, admittedly at its very worst in 1811 which was also a year of violent cyclical depression, was left unsolved until well after Napoleon's downfall. If one remembers that over and above the cost of maintaining the army the regime was faced with indemnities of two million pounds at Pressburg and three and three quarter million at Schönbrunn, it is hardly to be wondered at that traditional values went awry. Meanwhile the mandatory inclusion of Austria in the Continental System from 1809 onwards posed a further challenge to the flexibility of her economic outlook.

Destruction of the Holy Roman Empire

In the midst of all this the prestige of the dynasty was in tatters and indeed this was probably the thing that upset Francis most. To a man of his conventional values the bitterest experience of all was perhaps the destruction of the Holy Roman Empire by Napoleon. The Habsburgs had enjoyed the imperial title continuously since the fifteenth century with one brief interlude, 1742–5, only to see the ancient concept brushed away by the upstart Corsican in 1806. To the more realistic commentators this action only gave formal recognition to the decay of an already anachronistic institution and when the Congress of Vienna met in 1815 to put to rights the map of Europe, none could seriously press for the restoration of the Holy Roman Empire despite the general conservatism of the diplomatists present. As telling as any was the verdict of a young contemporary writer from Coblentz, Josef Görres, who in fact dated the demise of the Empire from the moment that the French Republic annexed the left bank of the Rhine:

On December the thirtieth 1797, at three in the afternoon, the Holy Roman Empire, supported by the sacraments, passed away peacefully at Regensberg at the age of 955, in consequence of senile debility and an apoplectic stroke.

Others dated the death of the Empire earlier still. Yet, however predictable the destruction of the Empire may have been, Francis witnessed its end with a heavy heart. He did his best to keep up some show of self-confidence by re-styling himself

Emperor of Austria and by keeping the initiative to the extent of declaring the dissolution of the Empire himself, rather than leave the announcement to Napoleon, but he was immensely saddened by the experience.

This then was the Empire that Metternich was summoned to save in 1809, a territorial unit that had been reduced and decimated, where morale was low, economic circumstances were strained and leadership forlorn. It was hardly an inviting prospect, for the failures of his predecessors could not be ascribed to any lack of variety in the solutions that they had attempted. Thugut's policy of facing the French alone had collapsed at Marengo in 1800. His successor, Cobenzl, had espoused caution and then in desperation war and had duly resigned after the disaster at Austerlitz. Then had followed the exciting but ill-fated 'nationalist' revival under Stadion, whose war of revenge had ground to a halt at Wagram. Now it was Metternich's turn and his very selection was in a sense a measure of the Emperor's desperation, for he was in many ways an unlikely choice for such a responsible position.

[2] METTERNICH'S CAREER TO 1809

His family background

Metternich's appointment in 1809 was surprising not only because of his comparative youthfulness but also because he was really something of an outsider. He came of a Rhineland family and was thus not born with the advantage of an automatic introduction to the life and contacts of the court at Vienna. Furthermore, when his family was driven out of the Low Countries by the advance of the French armies they were but one of many who scuttled to Vienna to compete for the limited number of favourable openings that the Emperor might have in his grant. It was thus no mean achievement to have caught the attention of the Emperor and to have impressed him to the extent of such major promotion.

Metternich was born at Coblentz in 1773. His father, Francis George, was a Count of the Empire and in 1791 he was appointed Imperial Minister in the Austrian Netherlands. No great intellect, being better suited to the boring chores of etiquette and ceremony involved in his job than to any brain work that might be required, he was a responsible enough father to his two sons and went out of his way to see Clement on the road to a sound career, difficult though his circumstances became when the family was expelled from its estates by the French. But it was Francis George's wife, the Countess Kagenegg, who was the more formative influence on Metternich. It was to her that he owed his more obvious qualities of good looks and general sophistication. His elegance and poise were not the artificial ritualism of the second-rate courtier, but the natural attributes of the son of this sensitive woman, and these qualities were to stand him in good stead later on as he schemed and manoeuvred in the highest European circles. Indeed one may sense just a tinge of admiration even in the carping Treitschke's comment that in the brilliant society attending the Congress of Vienna Metternich 'swam as happily as a fish in a glittering pool'.

The vision of his parents and their determination to give him the best possible credentials in the rat-race for favour, into which they were thrown when they arrived in Vienna in 1794, can be seen clearly in the marriage that they arranged for him the following year. His bride was Eleonore von Kaunitz, a granddaughter of Maria-Theresa's distinguished foreign minister. That this was a marriage of convenience is to a considerable extent true. The main object of the exercise was undoubtedly to secure the entry into the highest Viennese circles, to which the Metternichs' Rhineland background did not automatically entitle them. Furthermore, Metternich himself had already lost his heart to a flirtatious French duchess, whom he had met in Mainz and who was to be but the first of a series of mistresses whom he was to acquire in addition to three wives during his lifetime. Nonetheless the marriage worked quite well. Eleonore, whilst not being particularly attractive, was socially accomplished; she admired her husband and made the best she could of a marriage which was from the start devoid of strong emotion.

Meanwhile, Metternich had been developing a mind of his own. After periods of study at the universities of Strasbourg and Mainz, he had taken the chance in 1794 of going to England with a financial mission from the Austrian Netherlands. How far he was influenced by his contact with Burke during these months is debatable. What is clear, however, is that the combination of his own experience of the Revolution in Europe and his reaction to the relative stability which he saw and liked in England was serving to consolidate the conservative principles which were already inherent in his upbringing. He was developing an attitude of mind well orientated to win him the goodwill of the Emperor, should he get the opportunity of demonstrating his leanings to him.

Diplomatic service

His chance to start a diplomatic career came in 1801. Metternich appears not to have been unduly enthusiastic at the opportunity but, typically particular where his own interests were at stake, he reviewed carefully the three openings offered to him by the Emperor and chose wisely. Copenhagen he rejected as being too much out of the focus of current events. A post in the Diet of the Holy Roman Empire, as a representative for Bohemia, was uninviting and might well end up in redundancy. On the other hand the role of plenipotentiary to the Court of Saxony at Dresden was more attractive, facilitating as it did a closer look at one of the focal points of Napoleonic attention and offering at the same time the chance to meet and mix with diplomats of experience and distinction. Metternich therefore opted for Dresden.

From this minor start Metternich's diplomatic experience underwent rapid expansion. In 1803 he was posted to Berlin as ambassador and saddled with the unrewarding task of trying to induce the timid Frederick William III to commit his forces to action against France. Then suddenly there came his first major break. In the reshuffle following the defeat of Austerlitz Metternich was selected to replace Stadion as Austrian ambassador to St Petersburg; but because Napoleon was not prepared to accept Cobenzl as ambassador in Paris and because Metternich had made a good impression on one of Talleyrand's agents in Berlin, his posting to Russia was revoked and instead he found himself transferred to the Austrian embassy in Paris, there to strive after some kind of working relationship with the ogre, Napoleon. Metternich himself was not a little alarmed at the magnitude of the task thrust upon him, but far from proving his undoing this appointment was to have profound consequences, for it enabled him to study Napoleon at first hand and to draw his own conclusions as to Napoleon's more vulnerable characteristics. Then, within three years, he was on the move again, for in 1809 there came the Emperor's summons and Metternich made his way to Vienna to take up the position of Minister for Foreign Affairs, which he was to hold for the next thirty-nine years.

Metternich the Rhinelander, the outsider, had gained a chance to make himself indispensable to the Emperor and it was a chance that he was to take, for whereas his predecessors had failed in their various approaches to the French threat Metternich was to succeed and his success was to give him a place in the Emperor's confidence that he was never to throw away.

[3] METTERNICH'S CHARACTER

It is not at first sight easy to see why Metternich was able to achieve this remarkable and rapid rise to influence and prestige, for there were far too many obvious shortcomings in him to allow of the argument that he came to the top simply because he was too abundantly able to be denied. Indeed he had a host of irritating traits, which have aroused in more than one historian a passionate urge to vilify, ridicule, and decry.

Most provoking is probably the incredible vanity of the man.

There was about him a disconcerting tendency to find fault any-
where but in himself. The situation had been impossible from
the start, he would argue, or somebody somewhere had slipped
up and upset the smooth working of a plan which would otherwise have worked. In a letter which he wrote to his daughter,
the Countess Sandor, in 1849, he was still firmly putting the
blame elsewhere:

The first years of the nineteenth century found me on the field of
battle where I have fought during the past forty nine years without
deserting my flag. In this long period nothing has escaped me; I know
all that forms the history of this period and also, as a result, the
history of my public life. Well! I think that my own history is pre-
ferable to that of society during the first half of the century. A glance
at my life brings peace to my soul, but the sight of the world does
not do as much . . .

Earlier, in 1819, he had written, 'there is a wide sweep about
my mind. I am always above and beyond the preoccupations of
most public men; I cover a ground much vaster than they can
see, or wish to see. I cannot keep myself from saying about
twenty times a day, "how right I am and how wrong they are" ',
and he capped this in the same year with a letter to the Countess
Lieven which, even allowing for his natural desire to impress the
lady in question, leaves one gasping for breath:

I have long experience of the world's affairs and I have always
observed that no matter is so easily settled as that which appears to
present insuperable difficulties.

Against this kind of stunning self-confidence his other more
idiosyncratic shortcomings pale somewhat – his obsession with
his personal appearance, his clothes, his physical elegance and
such like; his inordinate snobbery, much vaunted; his numerous
affaires and so on. When totalled together these various features
do not spell out a giant amongst his fellows, striding inevitably
to success on his incontrovertible merit, but nor do they really
merit the blistering derision meted out by A. J. P. Taylor in his
amusing essay on Metternich in *Englishmen and Others:*

Vain and complacent, with fatuous good looks, his first thought in a crisis was to see whether his skin-tight breeches fitted perfectly and the Order of the Golden Fleece was hanging rightly. Even his love affairs – and he had many – were calculated for their political effect . . . it must have been disturbing when he whispered political gossip in bed. He never made a clever remark. His thoughts, like those of most conservatives, were banal and obvious. Things must get worse before they get better, after war Europe needs peace, everyone has his allotted place in society. Most men could do better while shaving.

Had Metternich been the fatuous mediocrity here depicted then his rise to power would be difficult indeed to explain. However, there was much more to the man than mere vanity and political opportunism. Above all, he was a cultured creature, possibly somewhat out of place in the hurly-burly of the nineteenth century – rather the 'beau ideal of the eighteenth-century aristocracy' as Dr Kissinger describes him – but a man of intellectual and artistic awareness. He took a positive interest in painting, in architecture and music, and there is a touching simplicity in a letter written to the Countess Lieven in 1818. In this he singles out music for special praise: 'nothing affects me like music. I believe that after love, and above all with it, it is of all things in the world the one which makes me a better human being'. There is too an engaging, if somewhat philistine, frankness in his reaction to novels:

Novels I never look at unless I am persuaded that they are classics having some literary value. The ordinary novel does not interest me: I find it always inferior to my own experiences. Powerful situations strike me as exaggerated and I cannot resist looking at the last page, in which the characters marry or get killed, at the same time as I look at the title. Then nothing is left but to say Amen and the novel is finished.

In fact, most of his leisure time reading was devoted to scientific topics and it was with science, especially medicine, that he was most involved when off duty. Indeed he frequently used medical imagery when illuminating political and social problems, as we shall see, and it was on Metternich's own motion that the Emperor Ferdinand established the Academy of Sciences

in Vienna in 1846. One may argue that these varied interests
were shallow, that they are typical of a man who never got to
the core of anything, but nonetheless there is a breadth of vision
here which is attractive. Probably his claim that he would have
preferred to develop his scientific interests rather than pursue
the diplomatic career that his parents had mapped out for him
was something of an affectation, but it is refreshing to find in
Metternich such variety and such sensitivity. And to cap it all
he was able to pursue these interests and to do his job properly,
because he was a thoroughly hard worker. Again it is in a letter
to the Countess Lieven that one finds a picture of his daily
routine. Under the circumstances a little exaggeration on Metternich's part might reasonably be anticipated, but the picture is
backed up time and again by other contemporaries.

Would you like to know how I live? This is it, the whole year round.
I get up between eight and nine o'clock. I dress and go to breakfast
with Mme de Metternich. There I find my children and stay with
them till ten. I go to my study and work or interview people till one.
If the weather is fine I go riding, returning at half past two, I work
until half past four. I go to my salon and invariably find eight, ten
or a dozen people who have come to dine. I go back to my study at
half past six. Nearly every day I visit the Emperor. I stay there a
good while and then back to work until between ten and eleven
when I move into my salon where social callers and strangers are
assembled. I say a word to the ladies and I retire at one o'clock.
Holidays, Easter, winter or summer I never change my routine.

[4] HIS AFFINITY WITH THE EMPEROR

That Francis should have turned to Metternich in his hour of
greatest need and agony of mind, after the defeat at Wagram,
can be explained simply enough at a superficial level. The policies
of his ministers to date had failed to halt the progress of Napoleon. What was more natural then than that Francis should turn

to the young diplomat who had made so staunch a showing in
the crucial post of Imperial ambassador to Paris? The man who
had seen so much of Napoleon at close quarters, had even made
something of an impression on Napoleon himself, might conceivably do better than his ill-starred predecessors in conducting
the Emperor's foreign affairs.

But there was more to it than this. The Emperor was tired of
the bickering and quarrelsomeness of his advisers, among them
his own brothers whose radical sympathies found no room for
development in the tightly conservative regime that Francis
represented, and in the psychological nadir that followed Wagram he needed more than ever a man on whose solidarity he
could rely. The reality of this yearning, perhaps subconscious at
the time, is amply vouched for by the fact that within a year of
Metternich's appointment as Foreign Minister the Archdukes
Charles, John and Rainer, had all been expelled from Vienna and
thus from effective influence on policy. Metternich was not responsible for this, but he made sure that they did not return
during his master's lifetime.

Metternich was for Francis something of a God-send. There
was a degree of harmony in their attitudes which, together with
a natural deference on Metternich's part, made for an easier relationship than Francis had ever enjoyed before. Nor is this
really surprising, for it is not overfanciful to see in the positions
of Metternich himself and of the Habsburg dynasty as it then
found itself a very real similarity making for a natural harmony.
Both were victims of the Revolution, both found themselves
bruised and battered by forces which challenged the essence of
their traditions, both sought above all the opportunity for re-
trenchment and restoration. Thus it was that each found in the
other consolation and incentive.

From 1809 Metternich and the Emperor worked together to
pick up the pieces of the crumbling Empire and to try to save
something from the wreckage. Metternich's own fortunes were
inextricably involved with those of the humbled Habsburg
dynasty, for Metternich could only secure his own position if he
could maintain the dynasty. On his success or failure hung both

his own career and the immediate fate of the Habsburgs. One can argue endlessly about Metternich's priorities – was he really interested, as he alleged, in the dynasty and the Empire as a European necessity or was he simply talking in this way to cover the nakedness of his own self-interest, which demanded a revival of Habsburg fortunes? But in the last resort this is an unrewarding dispute, for in most human beings principle and self-interest are inextricably inter-woven. There does, however, linger on one major query and that is whether or not Metternich might have risked more had his own future not been so involved with that of the Empire.

Both Metternich and Francis were firmly convinced that the only way out of their troubles was through a course of caution and conservatism. The revolution was to be held at bay, its insidious creed was to be barricaded out and the French usurper was ultimately, it was hoped, to fall victim to the revolutionary excesses implicit in his own regime. Metternich accordingly took the line that the Revolution was a peculiarly virulent but essentially local phenomenon which would pass and he went to great lengths to back his interpretation of the demands of the situation with a convincing philosophical structure, though his more determined critics might slyly suggest that the ultraconfident tone of his writing was intended to convince himself no less than his readers.

[5] METTERNICH'S POLITICAL PHILOSOPHY

The main body of Metternich's political philosophy was clearly formulated fairly early on in his career, for a comprehensive statement of his views can be found in the 'Political Testament' that he addressed to the Tsar in 1820. Although as time wore on he wavered from this in practice it does hold good as a statement of his guiding principles. In his philosophising Metternich was very much the child of the eighteenth century, despite his loathing of some of the extremer characteristics of 'enlightened' thought, the virulent anti-clericalism of Voltaire and the contractual philosophy of Rousseau. He saw the whole complex problem of good government as one which could be unravelled by the powers of 'reason'. There were certain fundamental laws, which were discoverable and which, if observed, would make for stability and tranquillity in society.

Just as the Physiocrats postulated a natural economic order, which if discovered and adhered to would make for economic contentment, so Metternich postulated a natural social order, which if discovered and adhered to would have similarly advantageous results. Thus the optimism of the eighteenth century was not entirely lacking in Metternich, though he was to become progressively more depressed, as decade followed decade, at man's failure to accept his vision and avail himself of the benefits of the 'natural order'. If only the malcontents would heed his logic, he implied, for his beliefs were firmly grounded in history. He was, he claimed, '*tout à terre tout historique*' and his remedies were no unobtainable vision. 'I am a man of prose', he insisted, 'and not of poetry'.

Since, in Metternich's view, the nature of man was unchanging, it was possible to lay down general rules for his guidance. Individual institutions would rise, flourish and then fall, as do individual organisms, but if man would bear in mind two fundamentals, 'which never cease to exercise their indestructible influence with equal power', he would maintain a harmonious relationship with 'nature'. First he must adhere to the precepts of morality, religious as well as social, and secondly he must adapt to the geographical requirements of his locality. Here too the eighteenth-century environment can be plainly seen, for the concern with morality is surely a reflection of Metternich's revulsion at certain of the excesses which followed from the anti-clericalism of the 'Enlightenment', whilst the concern for geographical features reflects his assimilation of an eighteenth century preoccupation first popularised by Montesquieu.

The history of mankind, as painted by Metternich in his 'Political Testament', is the history of tensions and conflicts – conflicts between states, conflicts between races, classes, creeds. But history proper, he contends, dates only from the advent of Christianity, for this it was which made the natural law meaningful. Now there was a 'pure and eternal law', 'applicable to all times and to all places', to which authority must conform. Now as never before was man given a yard-stick by which to measure his own performance. (Metternich's personal religious position is not easily established. He became increasingly pious with age, but one cannot help suspecting that his championship of the Christian law in these early years was basically utilitarian. The Church was an integral part of the established order that he was seeking to restore. This is not, however, to say that he was insincere in the stand that he took. Once again perhaps principle and self-interest are blurred together here?) Inevitably tensions still persisted, but from time to time man would achieve the periods of repose that were Metternich's ideal and in which there was an equilibrium of forces and thus a healthy measure of conformity to the 'natural law'. This equilibrium was Metternich's goal. In the words of E. L. Woodward, 'the basis of Metternich's philosophy was the idea of the balance of power as a cosmic principle'. In other words he sought repose in interstate rivalries, just as he did in domestic rivalries, through the balancing of those forces which were destructive by those which were not. In such a situation he looked not for immobility, but for cautious measured progress within the confines of the 'natural' order.

Unhappily, Metternich contended, there had been a marked and rapid deterioration of the ideal balance over the past three centuries. The sixteenth century had seen three discoveries whose combined effect had been devastating. The invention of printing had speeded up the communication of ideas, which was in itself no bad thing, but it had regrettably facilitated the better circulation of false ideas along with the good. 'If the same elements of destruction which are now throwing society into convulsion have existed in all ages – for every age has seen immoral and ambitious men, hypocrites, men of heated imagination, wrong motives and wild projects, yet ours, by the single fact of the liberty of the press, possesses more than any preceding age the means of contact, seduction and attraction whereby to act on these different classes of men'. Small wonder then that Metternich was a determined champion of censorship.

Second on Metternich's list of evils came the invention of gunpowder, which had revolutionised the whole strategy of attack and defence and exposed the concept of balance between communities to shocks of unprecedented violence. Last but not least there was the discovery of America, which had had profound effects on the old order both materially and psychologically. The sudden influx of precious metals into Europe had undermined the traditional view of landed property as the real source of value and the new opportunities for initiative and enterprise in the new world had stimulated unrest and dissatisfaction with things as they were in the old.

Thus it was that man had been rapidly seduced away from the old values to dream presumptuous dreams of a future which should conform not to the law of nature, but rather to the law of his own individual whim. 'Presumption' was to Metternich's mind the prime mover in man's recent catastrophes. Casting aside the dictates of reason and the observance of the natural law, men had presumed to re-mould the universe to their own requirements. The dramatic increase in human knowledge, which had followed the Reformation period had not been accompanied by an equal growth of wisdom, 'the only counter-poise to passions and to error'. In short, man had presumed on his function, which was to adapt to the unchanging laws which govern the universe and not to seek to tamper with them.

For substantiation of his theories, Metternich had not far to look. In the revolutionary turmoil from which Europe was just emerging, the bloodshed, the chaos, the instability, he found his proof that man was pursuing a false path. Revolution was fundamentally unsound as a method of change, he argued. Change, if it were to prove durable, must proceed slowly and out of an 'ordered situation'.

A consideration the liberal spirit usually ignores ... is the difference
in the life of states, as of individuals, between progress by measured
steps and progress by leaps. In the first case, conditions develop with
the consequence of natural law; while the latter disrupts this con-
nection .... Nature is development, the ordered succession of
appearances; only such a course can eliminate the evil and foster
the good. But leaping transitions wind up by requiring entirely new
creations – and it is not given to man to create out of nothingness.

An icy douche this for revolutionary ardour, if change can only
be satisfactorily achieved by the establishment, which is an
inference reasonably to be drawn from this statement.

Belief in cooperation between governments

How then was the natural order to be restored in a Europe still
seething with revolutionary aims, some but half formulated,
others trumpeted abroad with alarming confidence? This was
the crucial and immediate responsibility of the governments of
Europe, Metternich argued. 'We are convinced that society can
no longer be saved without strong and vigorous resolutions on
the part of the governments still free in their opinions and
actions'.

Respect for all that is; liberty for every government to watch over
the well-being of its own people; a league between all governments
against factions in all states; contempt for the meaningless words
which have become the rallying cry of the factions; respect for the
progressive development of institutions in lawful ways; refusal on
the part of every monarch to aid or succour partisans under any mask
whatsoever – such are happily the ideas of the great monarchs; the
world will be saved if they bring them into action – it is lost if they
do not.

In this clarion call for unity and cooperation between governments, Metternich was true to his own philosophy, for he saw in
relations between states a conflict of forces, just as he did in
their domestic affairs. Each state has its 'separate' or selfish
interests, but there are also interests which are 'general' to all
states. Happily, Metternich believed, the modern trend was for

states to draw closer together and to cultivate the biblical precept, 'do unto others as ye would they should do unto you'. The ideal situation was clearly one where these general interests subdued the provocative selfish interests of states, as Metternich hoped they would do in this situation, the great powers thus combining on the first priority of stabilising Europe rather than furthering the recent chaos by pursuing selfish and mutually unacceptable policies. 'The great axioms of political science proceed from the knowledge of the true political interests of all states.'

Having emphasised the responsibilities of the governments of Europe, he backed up his case by his analysis of the causes of the revolution in France. High in his list of causes comes 'the feebleness and inertia of governments'. Whilst many could see the disastrous way that things were going, governments, and especially the French, had done nothing to stop the trend. Indeed, the French government had foolishly given some token of approval to the sinister force afoot when it had aided the Americans in their revolution. And Napoleon himself, although in many ways a counter- revolutionary force, had inadvertently given the revolutionary legions in Europe a trump card to play. First of all he had thrown over tradition and then, as the peoples groaned under the demanding terms of Napoleonic rule, so revolutionary ideas had flowered and the revolutionary implications of such thinking had been obscured behind the general and respectable cloak of 'patriotism'.

Governments must be alert and wary. They had to understand the dangerous forces that they were up against. Cool analysis was a key component in Metternich's strategy. Likening revolution to a disease, he set out to understand it fully before prescribing a remedy. It was no solution to follow the example of those who, 'judging of a disease by its outward appearance, confound the accessory manifestations with the root of the disease and, instead of directing their efforts to the source of the evil, content themselves with subduing some passing symptoms'. So saying, Metternich set out to diagnose the root of the revolutionary malady.

Opposition to the Liberal idea

The spawning ground for the presumption, which he believed to lie at the root of man's recent agonies, he found in the middle classes of society, the *classe intermédiaire* as he called it. These were the people who had tasted success and rapid preferment, but were not yet satisfied and were eager for still more power and influence, their success to date breeding presumptuous aspirations for the future. The great mass of the people were too much involved with securing a livelihood to concern themselves with 'vague abstractions and ambitions' and were positively apprehensive of disorder, which would interfere with their daily employment. These were the 'real' people whom, Metternich argued, 'we find everywhere praying for the maintenance of peace and tranquillity, faithful to God and their Princes, remaining proof against the efforts and seductions of the factions who call themselves friends of the people and wish to lead them to an agitation which the people themselves do not desire!' That the vast majority of the aristocrats would oppose disorder was to be taken for granted, but Metternich slipped into his argument a reminder as to the likely fate of men in the higher strata of society who stepped out of line: 'their career is generally short. They are the first victims of political reforms and the part played by the small number among them who survive is mostly that of courtiers despised by upstarts, their inferiors, promoted to the first dignities of the state'.

It is on the middle classes then that the governments must concentrate. Their organisation must be dismantled, in particular the secret societies which are 'the gangrene of society'. Governments must be firm in resisting the claims of Liberalism and not pursue a weak policy of concession, which will merely stimulate further demands and a further departure from stability and order. They must beware the current rallying cry of faction, which is the word 'constitution'. In different regimes the word means different things, but everywhere it means 'change and trouble'. The Liberal Idea must be blotted out, for it is based on a misconception of drastic proportions. The middle classes look to gain power and influence for themselves, but what they fail to see is that they will not be able to stop the process they have begun.

Liberalism is but the accomplice of demagogy and serves, very often unconsciously, to drive a road for it and often to level that road most conveniently. Liberalism shares the fate of all fore-runners. Once the true lord appears it is almost impossible to find any trace of the fore-runner.

Metternich's hopes for the future

The programme that Metternich was demanding of the Great Powers then was one of concerted repression of a desperate and dangerous force. Conservatism was to be relentless and inflexible. 'One must not dream of reformation while agitated by passion: wisdom directs that at such moments we should limit ourselves to maintaining'.

However, Metternich was at pains to point out that this frozen attitude was not a life sentence. Revolution was like a contagious disease and the infection must be quarantined. Once the danger period had been lived through there would recommence a policy of construction. 'The governments in establishing the principle of stability will in no wise exclude the development of what is good, for stability is not immobility'. In these last words, 'stability is not immobility', Metternich sought to evade the charges of drabness, of lack of imagination, of obstructionism, which he shrewdly anticipated not only from the victims of his repressive policies but also from subsequent historians and commentators. His was not the doctrinaire conversatism of a Bonald or a de Maistre. Nor was he simply imposing an anachronistic system because it suited his or the Habsburgs' personal requirements. He was pinning his faith on the great monarchies, because they were the duly constituted authority of the time, they were a link in the natural chain of historical development to date. Now they would stand or fall by their ability to shape their policies in accordance with changing circumstances. It was their task to move cautiously with the times, but always within the confines of the natural law. This was the kind of measured change that Metternich regarded as 'natural' and therefore practicable. Let them make their priority the well-being of their peoples as a whole, let them not forsake their responsibilities in the weaker urge to make concessions to factions, and order might then re-emerge and with it the stability so earnestly desired by the 'real' people. This, and not factional rebellion, is the true road to freedom:

The word freedom has for me never had the character of a point of departure, but a goal. The point of departure is order, which alone can produce freedom. Without order the appeal to freedom is no more than the quest of some specific party for its special objectives and will in practice always lead to tyranny.

This then was the programme that Metternich developed and, needless to say, such sentiments as these found a ready listener in the Emperor Francis, whose reaction to the disasters of the Napoleonic period was to risk nothing and change nothing. That there was nothing exciting or stimulating about such a policy goes without saying and Metternich was clearly aware of the need to defend it vigorously for this very reason. The tantalising picture of the constructive conservatism which was to follow once stability had been restored was Metternich's justification for the negative quality of the policies of the moment. In 1815 there was much to be said for drawing breath for a moment or two. It was only later, as the tedium of repression seemed to become a habit rather than the promised temporary expedient, that Metternich's philosophy began to look more makeshift than commanding and the confidence of the man himself began to fray at the edges. Indeed there is something not a little pathetic about the way in which Metternich's early assertiveness disintegrates and becomes shot through with doubt as the years go by and the once vaunted confidence gives way to a series of pronouncements of Cassandra-type gloom. What happened to the constructive hopes of the earlier political writings? Was it that the philosophy was false or simply that Metternich lacked the constructive ability and the imagination to make the dream come true? These are questions to be kept constantly in mind as we look first at the successful out-manoeuvring of Napoleon and then at the attempts to restore to a position of eminence and stability the battered empire of the Habsburgs.

PART II
Napoleon's Downfall

[6] AFTER SCHÖNBRUNN

A comparison of the Habsburg position in 1810, after the signing
of the Peace of Schönbrunn, with that of 1815, after the signing
of the Vienna Settlement, reveals a staggering recovery in terms
of influence and prestige. For this recovery Metternich claimed
much of the credit and certainly he was very largely responsible
for the safe passage of Austrian interests during the last stormy
years of the Napoleonic period, though there were other factors
also instrumental in assisting the Habsburg interest, notably the
sympathetic diplomacy of Lord Castlereagh, the British Foreign
Secretary, and the general war-weariness of the Powers. This
exhaustion, coupled with various domestic problems, made the
Powers more amenable to a traditionalist settlement than they
might otherwise have been. The irony for Metternich, as was
later to become apparent, was that what seemed in 1815 a
glorious end to the troubles of an anarchic and revolutionary era
proved in fact to be but the beginning of an exhausting and
frustrating period of strife. In many ways 1815 was the climax
of Metternich's career and the period 1815–48 a disillusioning
postscript.

When Metternich became the Emperor's Foreign Minister in
1809, he inherited a depressing situation. Austria, having
gambled on the hope that the setbacks that Napoleon had experienced in Spain were the beginnings of broader reverses, had
been defeated. It was small comfort to know that the defeat had
not been as sweeping as that at Austerlitz. The morale of the

country and of the Emperor Francis were shattered and the terms of the treaty of Schönbrunn bore ample witness to the fact that Austria had shot her bolt. In short, whatever Metternich might have in mind, he had little room for manoeuvre for there could be no question of taking any action which might involve another costly and humiliating confrontation with the French. As Metternich himself insisted, there was no alternative to co-operation:

From the day that peace is made our system must be exclusively one of tacking, of obliterating ourselves, of accommodating ourselves to the victor. In this way alone we shall perhaps extend our existence until the day of general deliverance. Without the aid of Russia we must never again dream of shaking off the yoke which weighs upon the whole of Europe. That Court with its fluctuating spirit will awaken the sooner if it is no longer the only one to congratulate itself upon its wretched political conduct. Continually in contradiction with itself and with the principles it professed the day before, it will perhaps come and offer us its aid when it sees us follow in its track with the zeal of a rival. We have then but one course open to us; we must reserve our strength for better times and work out our salvation by softer means without regard for the road we have followed hitherto.

It was not to be a glamorous policy. Indeed it was to be a difficult one, for the process of accommodating the victor would almost certainly be misunderstood by ardent patriots and potential allies alike, but Metternich saw no alternative to hand.

In fact, the prospect of cooperation, at surface level anyway, was a less bitter pill for Metternich than for many. During his time in Paris he had seen a good deal of Napoleon and had come to admire a number of his qualities. Metternich respected the quickness of Napoleon's mind, his

extraordinary sagacity in appreciating causes and foreseeing con-sequences ... grasping the essential point, stripping it of useless accessories, developing his argument and only ceasing to elaborate when he had made his point perfectly clear and conclusive, always finding the right word or inventing one when the need arose, his con-versation was always full of interest.

Metternich admired too Napoleon's ability to assess people and noted with approval a shrewd remark about Talleyrand:

when I want to do something, I do not make use of the Prince of Benevento: I turn to him when I want to do nothing without appearing to want to!

Above all, as he was later to emphasise to the Tsar Alexander, Metternich admired Napoleon because he had 'tamed the Revolution', a feat which Metternich could applaud even in the parvenu Corsican. Indeed, had the question at issue simply been whether or not to allow the usurper Napoleon to remain in power in France, Metternich would have backed him unflinchingly for all his views about legitimacy.

What really concerned Metternich (and the Emperor) about Napoleon was the expansionist tone of his policies. It was plainly not to the Habsburgs' liking that the French should dismember their empire and to this understandable grievance Metternich added his own philosophic formula. The trend of Napoleon's policies was totally in conflict with Metternich's conviction that the peace and well-being of Europe could only be secured by the maintenance of equilibrium, a power balance. For Metternich balance was all: it was the key to domestic stability and it was equally the key to stability between states. Napoleon's bid for universal dominion must be balked and a balance re-drawn in Europe with France contained behind her natural frontiers, the Rhine, the Alps and Pyrenees, Russia behind hers, that is coming no further west than the river Niemen, and central Europe strong and controlled under the 'natural' authority of Austria and Prussia.

But how was this to be done, with Austrian resources at so low an ebb? Here Metternich hoped to exploit a weakness in Napoleon's character that he had noted when in Paris. Napoleon was basically insecure, Metternich believed, and he developed this theory in a cutting account of his first audience with Napoleon:

I found him standing in the middle of one of the reception rooms with the Minister for Foreign Affairs and six other members of his court. He was wearing his hat. This latter circumstance, improper in

every respect since the audience was not a public one, struck me as
uncalled for pretentiousness indicating the parvenu. I even felt like
putting my own hat on ... his attitude seemed to me to indicate
constraint and even embarrassment. His short squat figure, his negli-
gent appearance and yet at the same time his attempt to appear
imposing had the effect of undermining in me the feeling of grandeur
which one naturally associates with one before whom the world
trembles.

Metternich's account was perhaps biased, not surprisingly so
under the circumstances, but it did contain a considerable grain
of truth. Napoleon felt acutely that he was a parvenu and he
yearned earnestly for the sanctions of legitimacy to stabilise his
de facto supremacy. 'Few men', wrote Metternich, 'have been so
profoundly aware how precarious and fragile authority is which
lacks this foundation and how much it exposes one to a flank
attack.' It was this need that the Habsburg dynasty could supply
and whether or not the idea of the marriage of the Emperor
Francis's daughter, Marie Louise, to Napoleon was originally
Metternich's own or a French suggestion, Metternich siezed upon
it enthusiastically.

Napoleon's marriage

The marriage, which took place in 1810, was a superb start to
the necessary policy of accommodating the victor, whatever the
feelings of the unfortunate princess. Indeed it had a broader
significance too, for although it brought with it few obvious gains
in the short term – despite the fact that Marie Louise promptly
produced the son and heir that Napoleon had been hoping for,
a son with the blood of one of the oldest dynasties in Europe in
his veins, the most that Napoleon would grant to suffering
Austria was a small reduction in the Schönbrunn indemnity – the
long term benefits were considerable. It opened the way for the
second stage in Metternich's strategy, the surreptitious stimulation of a new anti-French alliance. The significance of the
marriage here was two-fold. Firstly, it lulled Napoleon's suspicions of Austria, for in his rather quaint conception of what

legitimacy involved he could never bring himself to entertain seriously the idea that his new father-in-law might actually be willing to sanction war against him. Secondly, it pointed to the impending breakdown of the Franco-Russian understanding that had been made at Tilsit, for Napoleon had looked first to Russia for a wife before turning away to Vienna.

The position of Russia was a vital issue for Metternich, for bitterly resentful of what he believed to have been Russian incompetence at Austerlitz and Russian treachery at Tilsit, Metternich nonetheless knew that no effective confrontation with France was conceivable without Russian participation. If Russia could now be led into open opposition to France and if she could be induced to commit herself irrevocably to a confrontation, then Metternich, behind the scenes, would spare no effort in encouraging others to join her. Russia, however, must be fully committed, for never again would Metternich run the risk of facing the French single-handed or even as the focal point in a coalition.

His plan then was clear. He must maintain the confidence of Napoleon; this was always the first priority. Then, in so far as was possible without alarming the French, he would do what he could to rebuild Austria's military strength, which was restricted by the terms of the treaty of Schönbrunn, and he would do his utmost to encourage effective cooperation against Napoleon, and to draw Russia forward as the driving force in a new coalition which Austria might ultimately join, but not until the element of gamble in such a move was reduced to a minimum.

There was, however, one major drawback to this strategy and it was a drawback that Metternich could see but could not escape. His ideal solution would probably have been for Napoleon, in face of mounting coordinated opposition, to accept a negotiated settlement in which he retained his power in France, but renounced all claims outside the natural frontiers. Such a decision would have been in accord with Metternich's concept of equilibrium and would have had the additional advantage of leaving France under firm rule and thus safe from revolution. The problem was that Napoleon's temperament was such that he could not be expected to negotiate or make concessions except in a situation of the direst military emergency. Indeed even this could hardly be counted upon, for Napoleon's conviction that his power at home was dependent on military success abroad might lead him to reject concession even in extremity on the grounds that a negotiated peace abroad would spell political suicide at home.

Whichever way Napoleon might choose to play it there was no escaping the one unquestionable truth that the Napoleonic threat to European, even world, repose could only be effectively countered by a monumental display of force. This, as Metternich rightly saw, involved the mobilisation of a really determined and effective coalition. But who was to say that all the members of such a coalition would see Metternich's equilibrium as the object of the exercise? Might not one Power or another seek, from a position of military strength, to pursue a selfish policy that was at odds with the equilibrium? It was not long in fact before Metternich came to see in Russia just this sort of threat. He was in a cleft stick, for given the temperament of Napoleon he must apply maximum military force to break the French preponderance and yet by allowing Russia to exert the pressure necessary to break Napoleon he ran the risk of substituting undue Russian predominance for the vanishing French imperium. Metternich's diplomatic skills were to be stretched to the utmost in the attempt to restore a genuine balance to Europe.

[7] CORNERING NAPOLEON

Metternich's chance to test Russian resolve came with the news of Napoleon's catastrophic retreat from Moscow. His policy was simple. He already had some sort of understanding with Alexander, for although the Austrians had had to contribute troops to the army that invaded Russia, Metternich had successfully ensured their safety by secret negotiations with the Russians whereby each side undertook to do the other as little damage as possible. Now he would see whether he could draw Alexander further west, testing that is to say his appetite for further pursuit of Napoleon. At the same time, Metternich would do his utmost to encourage others, Britain and Prussia in particular, to co-ordinate their efforts with Russia. Finally Metternich would take the first step in drawing Austria towards an independent position by seeking to get Napoleon's permission for Austria to play the role of mediator between France and her enemies.

Organising opposition to Napoleon

By a series of delicate manoeuvres Metternich was able to en-courage the development of organised opposition to the French, without in fact committing Austria to the extent of provoking Napoleon, though Napoleon's response to the idea of Austrian mediation was chilly at first.

In February 1813 he was able to reassure the Prussian govern-ment to such an extent that it forsook its enforced alliance with Napoleon and signed the Treaty of Kalisch with Russia. This, although not entirely palatable to Metternich, because it implied a Russian determination to take over Poland complete, did have the advantage of committing Russia further in the struggle against Napoleon. In February too Metternich sent Baron Wessenberg to London to urge the British government to accept Austrian mediation and to stress the advantages for Britain in a European equilibrium such as Metternich envisaged. At the same time Metternich embarked on a series of subtle military mano-euvres with the dual purpose of tightening Austrian defences and of encouraging Russian action. A series of contrived 'battles' were arranged with the Russians, giving Metternich the excuse to withdraw the Austrian auxiliary corps, first from the Vistula towards Cracow in January and then into Bohemia in March. By thus laying Poland open to Russian advance Metternich was able to test the Russians' determination. If they took their chance to move west, as in fact they did, then he would be able to place more faith in their intentions to go through with the reduction

of Napoleon. Napoleon meanwhile, although concerned at the
Austrian withdrawals, played further into Metternich's hands
by calling for the enlargement of the Austrian military establishment, which had been limited by the terms of Schönbrunn. Thus
Napoleon, eager for an effective Austrian contingent in the re-
formed Grand Army, in effect gave Metternich carte-blanche to
re-arm for his own purposes. It was here that Napoleon's conviction that the Emperor would not make war on his own son-
in-law began to redound so strongly to Metternich's advantage.

As the coalition against Napoleon gained in coherence, the
time was fast approaching when Metternich would have to
commit himself. The allies were beginning to become irritable
over the Austrian habit of sitting on the fence, the more so when
Napoleon won two good victories at Lützen and Bautzen in May
1813. Metternich himself realised that if Napoleon would not
accept reasonable terms Austria would have to join the war
effort, but such a decision would need the Emperor's agreement
and this was not going to be easily come by, since Napoleon's
May victories had served to remind the Emperor of past experiences at French hands. Metternich thus had no alternative but
to demonstrate to Francis that peace with Napoleon was impossible and this he set out to do by proving that Napoleon was
not prepared to make even the most reasonable concessions and
that war was therefore the only solution.

On 4 June an armistice was concluded between Napoleon and
the allies. It was to run until 20 July. On 27 June Metternich
signed the Treaty of Reichenbach with Russia and Prussia,
pledging Austria to join the war if she failed to get Napoleon's
agreement to four very moderate proposals: the dissolution of
the Grand Duchy of Warsaw, the enlargement of Prussia, the
return of Illyria to Austria and the restoration of Hamburg and
Lübeck as Free Cities. In this way Metternich set out to demonstrate to the Emperor, and indeed to all the world, that Napoleon
would not make even the mildest concessions and that this left
the allies no alternative but war. The fact that Napoleon had
every right to reject the terms on the ground that nothing was
said about what the allies would do if Napoleon did accept them

was to be glossed over, of course, though it is clear that the British Cabinet would not have regarded such concessions as adequate.

As far as Austrian commitment to the war was concerned all now depended on the forthcoming negotiations between Metternich and Napoleon. They met at Dresden on 26 June and Metternich has left to posterity a very graphic, if probably somewhat over-dramatised, account of the meeting. (In fact the account was not fully written up until 1829, so there had been time for Metternich's imagination to play its part, but the general tone of the account rings true.) In return for an extension of the armistice to 10 August, Napoleon agreed to release Austria from her French alliance and to accept her mediation. Detailed negotiations were to be deferred to a Congress, which was to meet in Prague on 10 July. Of considerable significance, if Metternich's account of the meeting is true, was Napoleon's explanation of his personal reaction to adversity, for this seemed to substantiate fully Metternich's suspicions that only total defeat would discipline his opponent:

Your sovereigns born on the throne may be beaten twenty times and still go back to their capitals. I, an upstart soldier, cannot do this. My reign will not survive the day when I cease to be strong and therefore feared.

Certainly Napoleon was not genuinely interested in a limited peace at this juncture, for he did not bother to send a plenipotentiary to Prague until a fortnight after the opening of the Congress there and then without any real powers of decision. The outcome was as abortive as Metternich had anticipated and on 11 August Austria therefore became one of the allies, pledging herself still more firmly by the Treaty of Teplitz on 7 September.

In the event Metternich seemed to have timed his entry well, for in October the allies inflicted a crushing defeat on Napoleon at Leipzig and drove the French back west of the Rhine for the first time since 1805. But Metternich was uneasy, for he had no desire to see an unacceptable degree of Russian influence in Central Europe as the price to be paid for the reduction of

Napoleon and clearly the further west the Russians came the
greater would be their bargaining power. In a desperate attempt
to stop the Russian advance Metternich made one more generous
offer to Napoleon, having achieved the backing of both Alexander and the inexperienced British Ambassador to Austria,
Lord Aberdeen. These terms, the Frankfort Proposals of November 1813, were in fact more than the British Cabinet could take,
for they offered Napoleon the natural frontiers of Alps, Pyrenees
and Rhine, that is to say they offered him Belgium, the French
occupation of which had spurred England into the Revolutionary
War in the first place. But Metternich was not concerned about
Britain at this stage, indeed he did consider the possibility of a
European peace without Britain. He was primarily concerned to
keep France limited but stable and to prevent further Russian
advances.

A prompt acceptance of the proposals by Napoleon might have
split the coalition, but, true to form, Napoleon was not really
interested in negotiating, save as a means of gaining time for
further armament. The chance was missed and Metternich was
left once more with the problem of Russian ambition.

Concern for European equilibrium

It was now more or less certain that the overthrow of Napoleon
would involve an invasion of France and the question was how
to prevent Alexander from trying to impose on France a government that would fall short of European requirements for he had
already suggested the replacement of Napoleon by Bernadotte,
a plan which looked to Metternich suspiciously like a move to
make a Russian satellite of France.

Surprisingly Metternich got the sympathy and support that
he needed from the most determined critic of his own Frankfort
Proposals. So alarmed were the British Government at the
generosity of Metternich's offer to Napoleon that they took the
unprecedented step of sending the Foreign Secretary to France
in person. This was Lord Castlereagh, who arrived in January
1814 and brought to the allied headquarters a shrewd and deter-

mined mind. Castlereagh was adamant that any terms offered to
Napoleon should not again include Belgium. Indeed he wanted
to see Holland and the Low Countries joined together as a barrier
against future French aggression. But at the same time he came
to sympathise with Metternich's concern for the European
equilibrium and to give him valuable support in curbing the
Tsar.

Steadily now the allied plans were consolidated. Once more
Napoleon was offered terms, this time the *Bases de Troyes* which
offered him the frontiers of 1792, that is to say the frontiers
before the outbreak of the Revolutionary War, but this time
there was no lull in the fighting. The war went on and Napoleon
failed to take the offer up. Meanwhile Castlereagh played a major
role in putting the alliance on a sounder footing by the terms of
the Treaty of Chaumont, which was signed on 9 March 1814.
Each of the Powers undertook to put 150 000 men into the field
against France, Britain pledged a subsidy of five million pounds
and the four Powers further pledged themselves to supply a force
of sixty thousand men against any French aggression over the
next twenty years. The whole tone of the alliance was becoming
more purposeful. Meanwhile the resolve of the French themselves
was dwindling, even if that of Napoleon was not, and on 30
March Paris fell, to be entered by the Tsar on the following day.

Metternich then had achieved the first part of his programme.
He had taken Austria out of Napoleon's control without provoking French retaliation and he had contributed to the reduction of Napoleon without which no revived equilibrium was
conceivable. Now ahead of him lay the major constructive
problem. Could the Powers concerned in the humbling of
Napoleon be brought to subordinate their particular interests
to the general, to deny themselves in the interests of balance
and stability?

[8] THE PEACE SETTLEMENT

Metternich was firmly convinced that the period of order and stability that he hoped to inaugurate in Europe could only come out of a peace settlement which all the major Powers believed to be just. This was what he meant by a 'legitimate' settlement, one that satisfied the powers and thus committed them to its upkeep by moral conviction rather than by force. An equilibrium should be established in which all concerned would be conscious of a vested interest. To this end Metternich envisaged a France restored to her traditional role beyond the Rhine and content in that role, a Central Europe whose stability was in the care of Austria and Prussia in willing cooperation and understanding, and a Russia acknowledging the river Niemen as her Western boundary. In this equilibrium the mutterings of insurgent nationalism had no place, for Metternich did not see either Germany or Italy as suited to statehood and anyway such nationalists as there were in Italy and Germany were in a minority. That Metternich's concept of equilibrium suited the Habsburgs is obvious but it is not surprising that there was a tendency to resort to tried expedients rather than experiment after so prolonged a period of upheaval.

Metternich was well aware, of course, that the task was likely to be difficult. He was already well informed about the trend of Alexander's suggestions to Prussia in the negotiations which had led up to the signing of the Treaty of Kalisch in February 1813. Here the Tsar had hinted at Russian ambitions in Poland, an idea in conflict with Metternich's desire to keep Russia as far east as possible, and had suggested that Prussia seek compensation in Saxony, a move which would seriously upset the balance in Germany. Alexander had also taken a dangerously individual line over the choice of a French government to replace Napoleon. Whereas both Metternich and Castlereagh had come down in favour of the Bourbons as having the moral strength of legitimacy and also as being able to accept quite easily the old frontiers since these had been the Bourbon frontiers of Louis XVI,

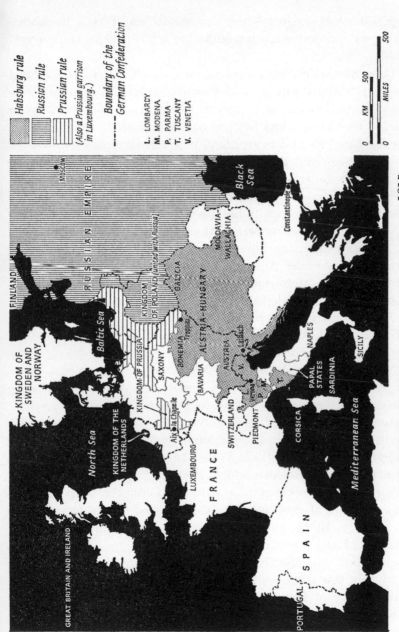

THE GERMAN CONFEDERATION AS ESTABLISHED IN 1815

(based on a map from *Europe 1789–1830* by Franklin L. Ford published by Longmans)

Alexander had suggested first Bernadotte and then a Republic, which was altogether too revolutionary a prospect for the current mood.

Thus Alexander, with Prussia very much under his shadow, looked a major obstacle to Metternich's plans. Nor indeed was Great Britain ideally sympathetic to his every wish, invaluable though Castlereagh had been in consolidating the alliance. The trouble here was that as an island power Britain was not unduly concerned with the finer sensitivities of the continental Powers. Castlereagh wanted an equilibrium quite as much as did Metternich, but he tended to be more cavalier over the extent to which traditional scruples might be ignored in achieving it. Thus for example he was less concerned than Metternich at the prospect of Prussia's annexing Saxony, for while they both wanted a strong centre under Austria and Prussia Castlereagh was less interested than Metternich in the distribution of power within that centre. For Castlereagh what mattered was simply that the European centre should be strong. For Metternich what mattered was not only that it should be strong but that Austria should be the dominant factor in that strength.

Nevertheless, in the months ahead it was again to be Castlereagh who stood closest to Metternich and it was predictably Russia and Prussia which were to cause him the most anxiety. Indeed the Tsar immediately put a foot disastrously wrong, for having entered Paris in triumph on 31 March, whilst Castlereagh and Metternich were still in Dijon, he went on to negotiate the Treaty of Fontainebleau which allowed Napoleon to keep his imperial title, provided him with an annual subsidy of two million francs at French expense and posted him to Elba in full sovereignty. By the time Castlereagh and Metternich arrived all was agreed and it was too late to reverse the decision which left Napoleon so dangerously close to the European mainland. Apart from this the settlement with France, which emerged in the First Treaty of Paris, was generally acceptable to Metternich. France was treated benevolently, being reduced simply to the Frontiers of January 1792 with a number of minor additions. She was allowed to keep the art treasures that had been taken from conquered countries by Napoleon and no indemnity or term of occupation was imposed. Thus it was hoped that, devoid of bitterness, France would fit smoothly and easily into the restored equilibrium under the trustworthy and traditional rule of the Bourbons. The broader European settlement was to be deferred to Vienna, though it was agreed in Paris that most of the former Austrian Netherlands would be joined with Holland to create an effective barrier against further French aggression (a British stipulation), that Germany would be reorganised as a Confederation and that Austria would be rewarded in Italy.

Congress of Vienna

When the Powers duly reconvened at Vienna in October 1814, the task facing Metternich was clear. The right of the victors to compensation was undeniable, but somehow they must be prevailed upon to tailor their demands to the primary requirements of the European equilibrium. It was clear too that the major conflict would concern central Europe, for France had already been dealt with and Britain came to Vienna with her acquisitive requirements generally met by a series of successful negotiations for naval bases and colonial outposts. Castlereagh was in Vienna not to gain territory for Britain but to ensure that the peace agreement that emerged was an adequate guarantee against the type of hegemony that had dominated Europe for too long.

In terms of compensation then the spotlight was on Russia, Prussia and to a lesser extent Austria, and the key to the settlement seemed to lie with Alexander, who had so far made no specific statement about his Polish demands. Much depended upon his attitude, for if he were prepared to restore to Prussia her former Polish possessions then Prussia's claims to compensation in Germany would be considerably weaker than if Alexander proved determined to hang on to them. In this case Prussia would have a strong case for consolidation in Germany, a thought not relished by Metternich. A series of discussions between Castlereagh and Alexander in October yielded two icy pieces of information, firstly that Alexander laid claim to almost all of the

Napoleonic Grand Duchy of Warsaw, much of it formerly Prussian territory, and secondly that he had no intention of giving way. This information was the more forbidding in that Alexander already had troops in Poland. His solution to the problem of Prussian compensation was that Prussia should annex Saxony, whose unfortunate ruler had been a little late in changing sides in 1813.

For Metternich this was a dire situation. He had no desire to see Russia so far west, indeed her proposed frontier would be less than two hundred miles from Vienna. Nor did he wish to see Saxony added to the central lands of the Hohenzollerns lest they gain undue predominance in Germany. His position was further jeopardised by the fact that although Castlereagh, his main ally, was opposed to the Russian consolidation in Poland, he was not particularly hostile to the idea of a stronger Prussia, for this would add to her effectiveness as one of the frontier buffers that he favoured for the future containment of France. Thus Metternich was at this stage virtually isolated on the issue of the Prussian annexation of Saxony.

On 22 October Metternich embarked upon an extremely cunning stratagem which, had it succeeded, might have solved the problem in a way much to his liking. In response to a memorandum despatched by Hardenberg on 9 October, suggesting that Prussia would support Austria and Britain in combating the Russian claims to Poland in return for permission to occupy Saxony, Metternich replied on 22 October that Austria would sanction Prussian occupation in the event of opposition to Russia proving *successful*. So far, so good – a fair compromise it would appear, for Metternich was apparently prepared to accept one or other of the evils implicit in the Russian stand, but not both. However, Metternich had a further veiled card in reserve, for if opposition to Russia *were* successful and Prussia duly regained her Polish territories, her claim to Saxony would be so greatly weakened, that it might well be dismissed by the Powers, not to mention the various German states, as unnatural aggrandisement. This being so, Metternich still had a chance of foiling both Russia and Prussia.

For a moment there looked to be a chance of success. With Alexander now temporarily isolated, Castlereagh got Austria and Prussia to join Britain in an ultimatum to the Tsar on 23 October. If Alexander would not negotiate on Poland, then the matter must be brought before the whole Congress. (So far all major dealings had been in the hands of the Big Four.) At last it seemed that there was a clear majority within the Four but it did not last long, for Alexander succeeded in winning back the King of Prussia in a stormy interview and on 5 November Hardenberg was ordered to withdraw from the counsels of Metternich and Castlereagh. Metternich retaliated rather later with a letter of the 10 December in which he formally denied the Prussian claim to Saxony. Once again deadlock had been reached, for the rapprochement of Prussia and Russia meant that the terms were once again the unpalatable double of the Grand Duchy of Warsaw for Russia and Saxony for Prussia and the four Great Powers were split down the middle on the issue.

Inclusion of France in the deliberations of the Powers

It was now that Metternich and Castlereagh reaped a rich reward for their insistence on a Bourbon restoration, for since France was in every way a legitimate Power once more why should she not be allowed a more positive role in the peace negotiations? What better way to break the deadlock than to invite Talleyrand, the French Foreign Minister, into the meetings of the Big Four? This would suit Castlereagh in that it would give him a majority against Russian demands in Poland. It would also suit Metternich both on that score and because he well knew that Talleyrand would be sure to oppose any radical aggrandisement of Prussia, for it was in the very nature of French diplomacy to oppose any undue consolidation of power in Germany. On 31 December Castlereagh and Metternich proposed that the Big Four should become the Big Five and when Prussia in a last desperate fling threatened war the new trend was further consolidated on 3 January, when Britain, Austria and France went on to sign a defensive alliance.

This was the high moment of crisis for Metternich but one that he handled with great tact, for the discomfiture of Prussia had been achieved without reference to purely Austrian interest, which would have reduced the issue to the level of a selfish squabble, but on grounds of European necessity. By leaving most of the talking to Castlereagh and to Talleyrand, Metternich had won a major point for Austria; he had also made some ground towards the kind of equilibrium that he had in mind.

The energies of the triple alliance had, in fact, done more than discomfort Prussia. They had impressed the all-important Alexander. He had little desire to go to war on Prussia's behalf. After all he was unassailably in command of Poland, which was his real concern. On top of this, always a man of rapidly changing moods, he was also at this time profoundly influenced by the radical Christianity of Baroness von Krüdener and her insistence on the value of the Christian virtues as a guide to policy-making no less than as a key to personal conduct. His intransigence gave way to a new benevolence and a policy of limited concession, which made a compromise solution possible.

Prussia was given Posen and the city of Thorn, which controlled the middle Vistula. (These two cities and the lands attached to them amounted to roughly one sixth of the Grand Duchy of Warsaw.) In return she was prevailed upon to accept rather less than half of Saxony, renouncing her claim to Leipzig in the south. On top of this and in accordance with Castlereagh's policy of surrounding France with strong barriers she was allocated a considerable amount of territory on the left bank of the Rhine. So the main problem was solved. Russia was firmly ensconced in Poland, but not as completely as had originally seemed likely. Prussia retained a foothold there and was restored to considerable influence in Germany. Thus a policy of general flexibility and concession had led to a workable solution. How perfectly balanced the solution might prove remained to be seen, but at least it was a far cry from the alarms of December 1814.

From Metternich's point of view the vital thing was that agreement had at last been reached without recourse to force and, what was more, Austria, who had had to compromise over

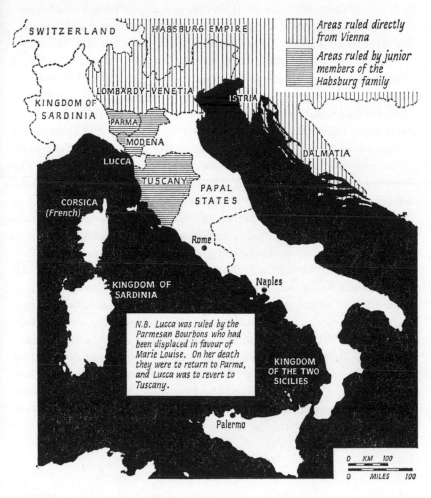

N.B. Lucca was ruled by the Parmesan Bourbons who had been displaced in favour of Marie Louise. On her death they were to return to Parma, and Lucca was to revert to Tuscany.

ITALY AFTER THE VIENNA SETTLEMENT

Poland and Saxony, had not gone unrewarded either. Admittedly she had lost the Austrian Netherlands, but these had been beyond her resources to control. She had also lost her share of the 1795 partition of Poland but on the other hand she had retained Galicia and the District of Tarnopol in Poland, she had regained Istira and Dalmatia on the Adriatic coast and she had achieved a position of dominance in Italy, where a new kingdom of Lombardy–Venetia was placed under the direct rule of the Emperor, the Duchy of Tuscany was restored to his brother, the Duchy of Parma went to his daughter Marie-Louise, and the Duchy of Modena to his grandson. Thus in the eight-state structure of Italy the Habsburgs had a substantial holding. The 'national' idea being thus defeated in Italy, so it was in Germany where a Germanic Confederation was instituted, consisting of thirty-four princes and four free cities and under the presidency of Austria.

In general Metternich had good reason to be satisfied. The heretical idea of nationalism had been thwarted and Europe remapped on a basis of equilibrium between the traditional States. To Metternich such a solution was a matter of principle, to others perhaps no more than a matter of common sense reliance on tried ideas in a time of revolutionary instability. But other people's motives were not of immediate concern to Metternich at this stage; what really mattered was that here was an equilibrium in which every State, whatever sacrifices it had had to make, had reasonable cause for satisfaction. Russia had moved substantially west, Prussia had gained in Germany, Austria had gained in Italy, Britain had seen established the safeguards against further French aggression that she required and France had benefited by the generosity of the Peace of Paris. Thus to a considerable extent the settlement was based on good-will and likely to be the more durable as a result.

Powers unite against Napoleon

The unanimity of the Powers was rapidly put to the test. The escape of Napoleon from Elba in March 1815 brought a prompt and effective response from the allies and almost more encouraging than this was the fact that few responsible Frenchmen showed any inclination to rally to the Emperor's standard. Nonetheless, the defeat of Napoleon in June did pose problems, encouraging though it was. It was axiomatic to Metternich, as it was to Castlereagh and Wellington, that France should be able to play an effective role in the European balance. Napoleon's escapade made it more difficult for her to do this, because it emphasised the lack of positive support in France for the restored Bourbons and it also evoked demands for a tougher peace settlement, notably from Prussia. The Second Treaty of Paris was not particularly harsh (and most of the credit for this should go to Castlereagh for even Metternich lost his composure at the peak of the crisis and demanded the reduction of French frontier fortifications), but it did not make the Bourbon task any easier by reducing the French frontiers more exactly to those of 1790 and by imposing an indemnity and an army of occupation. If it was encouraging to find the allies who had quarrelled so vehemently in December 1814 firmly united once more, it was nevertheless a pity that France could not embark upon the period of peace with the maximum advantages of the earlier treaty.

[9] THE NEW EUROPE

With Napoleon, the epitome of revolutionary presumption, at last consigned to a suitably distant confinement on St Helena, the Emperor Francis and his Foreign Minister could draw breath and review the Habsburg position. The situation was still uncertain, of course, most notably in Poland where Metternich turned anxious eyes lest the unpredictable Alexander unleash the forces of revolt again in an ill-considered orgy of liberal experiment, which could only have alarming repercussions in the areas of Poland still under Prussian and Austrian control. But as far as the Habsburg possessions as a whole were concerned a notable recovery had been staged, both in terms of territory and of prestige. Indeed, a certain magnanimity could be claimed on behalf of the Emperor who had voluntarily renounced his claim to the Austrian Netherlands and to the ancient title of Holy Roman Emperor, whilst at the same time material requirements had been satisfied by the recovery of the Tyrol and of Galicia, the Austrian presidency of the new Germanic Confeder-

EUROPE AFTER THE VIENNA SETTLEMENT

ation and her predominance in northern Italy. It was an achievement all the more remarkable for the fact that Metternich had had always to consider the ultra-timorous disposition of the Emperor Francis before committing himself to any opposition to Napoleon whatsoever.

For Metternich himself the outcome of the Vienna negotiations was doubly pleasing in that the settlement satisfied both the Emperor's concern for Habsburg power and prestige and his own formula for the future stability of Europe. However, he was shrewd enough to see that the Habsburg commitment in the new structure was a highly exacting one, for Germany and Italy were both areas with long past histories of instability and both had in the recent struggle experienced nationalist tremors which would need careful watching, for although the nationalist appeal had stirred but a few its contagious properties were an unknown quantity. Furthermore, trouble spots such as these had divided the Powers in the past and might well continue to attract the attention of any power whose concern for aggrandisement proved stronger than its dedication to stability. In short, if the equilibrium was to be maintained, the Habsburgs would have to accept a considerable responsibility for those areas, even to the extent of military intervention if necessary.

In his approach to this problem, Metternich came back to his idea of a legitimate equilibrium. The possible difficulties in Italy and Germany could be surmounted easily enough, provided that the Powers remained dedicated to the Vienna structure, for in guarding the stability of Italy and Germany, Austria was in fact guarding the Vienna settlement and could look to the other Powers for support, if necessary. Only in the event of one or more of the Powers abandoning the Vienna concept of European balance would Austria be dangerously exposed in her dealings with the trouble spots within her sphere of influence. The revised Habsburg structure was a vital part of the new equilibrium. Metternich's task was to maintain the loyalty of the Powers to that equilibrium, for their loyalty was a guarantee of Habsburg survival.

The Quadruple Alliance

Although Metternich never shed completely his uneasiness about the other Powers – the expansionist tendencies of Russia, Prussia and France and the insular irresponsibility of Great Britain – he nonetheless had some cause for optimism as he looked forward into the future at the end of 1815. There were grounds, both theoretical and practical, for thinking that the acquisitive instincts of the Powers had been blunted by the Napoleonic experience. The most tangible security, to Metternich's mind, was Castlereagh's Quadruple Alliance, which was signed by Britain, Austria, Russia and Prussia on 20 November 1815. This document was the logical expression of an understanding between these four Powers which had been established in the Treaty of Teplitz of September 1813, tightened in the Treaty of

Chaumont of March 1814 and consolidated in the stresses which
had led up to the signing of the Vienna Settlement in June 1815.
By its terms the Powers pledged themselves to action should the
territorial provisions of the Second Treaty of Paris be violated
or Napoleon make any further move to re-establish himself. To
this end each Power agreed to supply up to sixty thousand
troops to supplement the army of occupation, if necessary. Then,
as a further safeguard for the future, Article VI provided for
periodic meetings between the Powers to maintain the treaty
and to consider 'measures which shall be considered the most
salutary for the repose and prosperity of nations, and for the
maintenance of the peace of Europe'. Thus was born the Congress
System, on which Metternich pinned his hopes for future peace
and stability until it foundered on rival interpretations of what
constituted just grounds for general intervention. Disappointing
though the ultimate failure of the Congress System was, Metternich found much to admire in the Quadruple Alliance, particularly the assumption of a common interest and the expectation
of regular cooperation.

The Holy Alliance

Less welcome to Metternich was the Tsar's Holy Alliance, which
was signed by all the monarchs of Europe, save for the Pope, the
Turkish Sultan and the British Prince Regent. By contrast with
Castlereagh's clearly defined and practical document, the Tsar's
was vague and woolly in the extreme. Powerfully under the influence of his current religious enthusiasm, which was assiduously
fanned by Baroness von Krüdener, the Tsar sought to solve the
problems of peaceful coexistence between states by the application of Christian principles. In a spacious introduction to the
treaty Alexander declared his convictions.

Their Majesties, the Emperor of Austria, the King of Prussia and the
Emperor of Russia, in view of the great events which the last three
years had brought to pass in Europe and in view especially of the
benefits which it has pleased Divine Providence to confer upon those
states whose governments have placed their confidence and their

hope in him alone, having reached the conviction that the policy of
the Powers, in their mutual relations, ought to be guided by the
sublime truths taught by the eternal religion of God our Saviour,
solemnly declare that the present act has no other aim than to manifest to the world their unchangeable determination to adopt no other
rules of conduct, either in the government of their respective countries
or in their Holy Religion, than the precepts of justice, charity and
peace. These, far from being applicable exclusively to private life,
ought on the contrary directly to control the resolutions of Princes
and to guide their steps as the sole means of establishing human
institutions and of remedying their imperfections.

The treaty then proceeded to bind all the signatories to generous
cooperation under the only true sovereignty, which was that of
Jesus Christ. What really worried Metternich about the document was not so much that it looked so impractical as that much
of it had a dangerously egalitarian flavour. This fact, coupled
with his knowledge of the Tsar's liberal plans for Poland, made
him unwilling to accept the Holy Alliance.

However, there were advantages in keeping the Tsar amiable.
Metternich, therefore, although thoroughly cynical about the
document, prevailed upon Francis to sign it, but only on condition that certain passages were reworded. Metternich duly
ironed out the phrases that were capable of radical interpretation
and Francis signed. With this manoeuvre both sides were content, for Alexander, who had probably not the sensitivity of
Metternich to radical textual ambiguities, was happy with the
revised version of the treaty and Metternich and Francis were
willing to play the Tsar's game, if it meant putting him under
further obligation to his fellow sovereigns. As Castlereagh explained in a letter to Lord Liverpool on 28 September 1815, the
Emperor was unwilling to thwart the Tsar 'in a conception
which, however wild, might save him and the world much
trouble, so long as it would last'.

These then were the paper guarantees for the future, one much
to Metternich's liking, the other of no great value except in so
far as the Tsar might interpret it as a brake upon himself. There
was, however, another factor in Metternich's favour as he sought

to assess the chances of peace and stability. This was an altogether more material consideration than the paper agreements already discussed, for greatly in Metternich's favour was the fact that all the Powers were in real need of a period of repose for purposes of recuperation and domestic consolidation. They were unlikely to favour adventurous foreign policies as a result.

The general problem was that the economies of the Powers concerned in the Napoleonic wars had undergone considerable strain and the prospect of demobilisation looked likely to increase the tension and threaten serious unemployment. On top of this, there were particular problems. The Bourbons in France had seen an already difficult task made immeasurably more so by the Hundred Days. Whereas in 1814 they had returned to a France that was more apathetic than positively hostile, they had in 1815 to face a country which had just committed itself once more to a positive taking of sides on the issue of Bourbon rule. Conciliation was going to be more difficult now. In Prussia the King was faced with the relics of the nationalist enthusiasm of 1813 and also the major problem of how to coordinate his scattered dominions and commend his protestant rule to his new Rhineland subjects who were predominantly catholic. In Russia Alexander too had security problems in that he was far from the popular hero that he had sought to be in Paris and he had also to implement the settlement in Poland. Thus Metternich could reasonably assume that domestic preoccupations would blunt the urge for dynamic foreign policies, always provided of course that the duly constituted authorities could in fact hold their own with the domestic opposition. If they could not, then Metternich's legitimate order was an illusion.

Over-all then the prospects were encouraging. An equilibrium had been forged at Vienna, the 'unnatural' force of nationalism had been trodden under and there looked to be a real chance that the Powers concerned in maintaining the balance would combine effectively to do so. It was the aim of Metternich's diplomacy to keep the Powers loyal to the spirit of Vienna for as long as he possibly could, thereby securing the needs both of Europe and of the Habsburg Empire.

Metternich never doubted for an instant that his twin goals of
European repose and Habsburg stability on the basis of the
Vienna Settlement were compatible, indeed interdependent.
Others might perhaps argue, however, that, although Austria
certainly had a major role to play, Metternich might have seen
the equilibrium rather differently, had he not been so obsessed
by the need to please his Habsburg master, and that he would
have done better to saddle the Habsburgs with a smaller responsibility, better suited to their limited resources. Would it
have been more realistic, for example, to allow Prussia the kind
of consolidation that she sought in the annexation of Saxony and
accept that Austria's role lay outside Germany? Or should the
interest in Italy perhaps have been surrendered?

If in his determination to give Austria a major role in the
European balance he perhaps overplayed his hand, Metternich
stuck firmly to his task, for in the years that followed he strove
with all his energy to maintain the status quo by keeping the
Powers loyal to the settlement, curbing their acquisitive instincts
and ensuring that they would be prepared to rally should Austria,
or any other Power, experience serious difficulties within her
own sphere of influence.

However, this policy was no more than half a solution, whether
his first priority was in fact the Habsburg interest or the equilibrium or genuinely both simultaneously. Great Power solidarity
might help to keep the disruptive forces within the Habsburg
Empire at bay, but it was not a real solution. It was at best a
holding action that Metternich was fighting with his diplomacy.
What was vitally needed was a constructive policy for the refashioning of the internal bonds which held the Habsburg
Empire together. A more meaningful relationship must be forged
between Vienna and the Provinces. The Empire must be fur-
nished with a creative image; it must convince its various members that the alternatives to Habsburg rule were unattractive by

comparison with its benefits. Only then would the Empire be secure. Without a dynamic policy at the centre, the maintenance of a sympathetic Europe was little more than a delaying tactic whose effectiveness must in time deteriorate.

That Metternich understood this is clear. That he found the prospect daunting is hardly to be wondered at. In the long run it was to be his misfortune that he was more successful in the secondary tactic of diplomatic bargaining (see Part III) than in the solution of the domestic problem (see Parts IV and V) which was ultimately the sine qua non of success. His own plaintive remark that he ruled Europe sometimes, but Austria never, furnishes fitting comment on the difficulties that he experienced in the postwar period.

Principal Events, 1812-15

THE CONSOLIDATION OF THE FOURTH COALITION

1812. Britain at war with Napoleon since 1803.
24 June. Napoleon crossed the Niemen to invade Russia
July. Formal Russian alliance with Britain

1813. 28 February. Prussia joined Russia in Treaty of Kalisch
27 June. Austria agreed to join the war if Napoleon would
not accept terms. Treaty of Reichenbach
11 August. Austria declared war on France
9 September. Austria further committed to Russia and
Prussia by the Treaty of Teplitz. Undertook not to
conclude a separate peace

1814. 9 March. Treaty of Chaumont coordinated the war effort
of the four Powers and pledged them to twenty years'
solidarity against further French aggression

1815. March to June. The Hundred Days
26 September. The Holy Alliance of the Tsar by which the
signatories undertook to apply Christian principles to affairs
of state
20 November. The Quadruple Alliance guaranteed the new
frontiers of France and laid down machinery for further
meetings (Article VI)

OFFERS OF PEACE AND THE ACTUAL PEACE TREATIES

1813. November offer (The Frankfort Proposals). Metternich
offered Napoleon the natural frontiers

1814. 17 February. The 'Bases de Troyes'. Four Power offer,
coordinated by Castlereagh – frontiers of 1792
13 April. Treaty of Fontainebleau sent Napoleon to Elba in
full sovereignty
30 May. First Treaty of Paris more or less confirmed the
'Bases de Troyes'

1815. 9 June. The Vienna Settlement signed in full Congress
20 November. The Second Treaty of Paris cut France back
to the frontiers of 1790 and provided for an army of
occupation and the payment of an indemnity

PART III
Metternich and Europe

[11] OBSTACLES TO SOLIDARITY

Metternich's concern to uphold the Vienna structure in Europe was a matter of principle, in that the settlement represented to him a just equilibrium, and a practical necessity, in that the revived Habsburg Empire needed time to put its house in order, free from the fear of outside interference. The longer the Powers could be prevailed upon to honour both the spirit and the letter of the settlement, the longer would be the period of European repose and the greater the chance of making the Habsburg Empire a going concern once more. To the task of binding the Powers together in defence of the conservative principle Metternich brought resourcefulness, perseverance and considerable diplomatic skill, though in the long run he was to find it a task beyond his means. Despite the apparent unanimity of the Powers, when Napoleon's unwelcome return had put it to the test, the task of keeping them together was not likely to be an easy one, for there were clearly discernible obstacles to cooperation both in the short term and in the long.

The long-term problem was obvious. Once the exhaustion of the war effort had been surmounted, the other Powers might well decide that they had more to gain than to lose by deserting the present equilibrium and pursuing once more their own selfish interests. This fear related more to the continental Powers than to Britain. Britain at least had a permanent interest in European stability, even though she might be unduly casual about how that stability were secured, but the other Powers had powerful temptations before them. Prussia was now so straddled across Northern Germany that there must be a logical urge to consolidate further. Russia's tradition of westward expansion had been dramatically consolidated at Vienna and might not yet be satisfied. France must in time develop some kind of desire to recover prestige and perhaps even territory. All of these Powers would need shrewd and careful handling if the Vienna equilibrium was to survive and the selfish and particular interests of the states were to be subordinated to the general interest, as Metternich saw it.

Differences amongst the Powers

The immediate problem was that, although there was a general concern for peace and stability in 1815, there were serious differences amongst the Powers as to how that stability could best be maintained. To Metternich himself there was little doubt about this. The territorial structure of Vienna should be regarded as sacrosanct and guaranteed by the threat of corporate intervention. What was more, there must be solidarity between governments against the forces of revolt and unrest in Europe, wherever they might erupt, for not until these were subdued could any kind of progress be seriously considered. Only through Great Power solidarity could the revolutionary virus be exterminated.

Britain

Unfortunately for Metternich neither Britain nor Russia, probably the two most crucial members of the Quadruple Alliance, saw things quite so simply. Britain had always been an unreliable sort of ally from the continental standpoint. Being less immediately involved, she tended to commit herself less readily. On both aspects of Metternich's programme the British Cabinet and the British public were likely to prove awkward. There was a marked reluctance in Britain to get involved on the continent save in cases of a really major threat to the European balance, such as had brought Elizabeth into the war with Spain in the 1580s, William into the war with France in the 1690s and Pitt into the war with revolutionary France in 1793, and so it was predictable that no British Cabinet would commit itself to so dogmatic a programme of intervention as Metternich proposed. The most that might be hoped for was that in the event of a really serious challenge to the Vienna equilibrium, rather than an insignificant and minor sideshow, then Britain might feel obliged to commit herself on behalf of the status quo. Even Castlereagh, who had a far more progressive concept of the contribution that Britain might make to European stability than had the Cabinet, was not to be swept away in Metternich's comprehensive approach. In his State Paper of 5 May 1820 he made a classic statement of the British position:

we shall be found in our place when actual danger menaces the system of Europe; but this country cannot and will not act upon abstract and speculative principles of precaution. The alliance which exists had no such purpose in view in its original formation.

If Britain was unlikely to act against attempts at territorial aggrandisement unless they constituted something approaching a bid for European hegemony, it was even less likely that she would be prepared to intervene against revolutions within the states and directed against the conservative social order, for it was hardly to be expected that a self-consciously constitutional state would lend force to block liberal developments elsewhere and besides this there was a strong British tradition against interference in the internal affairs of other states. Thus Castlereagh, although himself profoundly aware of the social peril in Europe, could not, even if he would, give Metternich any broad guarantee that Britain would back his policies by force. In a letter of December 1815 to the British Ambassador in Berlin Castlereagh emphasised that Britain's role was to persuade rather than to coerce:

in the present state of Europe, it is the province of Great Britain to turn the confidence she has inspired to the account of peace, by exercising a conciliatory influence between the Powers, rather than put herself at the head of any combination of Courts to keep others in check. . . . The immediate object to be kept in view is to inspire the States of Europe, as long as we can, with a sense of the dangers they have surmounted by their union, of the hazards they will incur by a relaxation of vigilence, to make them feel that the existing concert is their only perfect security against the revolutionary embers more or less existing in every State of Europe; that their true wisdom is to keep down the petty contentions of ordinary times, and to stand together in support of the established principles of social order.

It was ironic that the Foreign Minister in whom Metternich had the greatest confidence was the one with the least freedom of action, saddled as he was with a direct responsibility to an elected parliament.

Russia

The Russian problem was of quite a different nature. Indeed whereas Metternich's problem with Britain was the fear that she would fail to lend weight where it was needed, his problem with Alexander was to prevent him from an over-enthusiastic pursuit of intervention. In one significant way, however, the Russian problem was simpler than the British. Metternich knew that he could never control British foreign policy, because even if he could dominate the British Foreign Minister he could never master the Parliament to which that minister was ultimately responsible. Alexander on the other hand was answerable to nobody, for Metternich was convinced that Russian society was far too uncultivated to exercise any real control over the Tsar. The Russian Court he despatched as 'that quagmire of half-men, composed of the vilest substances but gilded on all sides, thirty-six carat ignorant and bloated like so many balloons, running after fashion and yet only making themselves ridiculous'. Thus, if he concentrated all his efforts on Alexander he might come to dominate Russian foreign policy to a real extent.

But Alexander was not an easy man to control. That he was intelligent, Metternich had no doubt, but it was a wandering intelligence without any real stability or fixity of purpose. Alexander's would not be an easy mind to harness. In a letter of August 1817 to Prince Esterhazy, his ambassador in London, Metternich recalled a saying of Napoleon: 'it would be difficult to have more intelligence than the Emperor Alexander has, but it seems to me that there is a piece missing and I cannot discover which'. Metternich's letter developed this idea:

since then I have twenty times been in a position to observe the aptness not only of the observation, but of the very expression Napoleon used. Today I am convinced of the truth of it, and if a doubt still lingers it is that of wondering whether in a particular circumstance, there is a piece missing or a piece too many.

In a portrait of the Tsar, which he wrote subsequently in 1829, Metternich looked further into the Tsar's erratic character and commented on the 'periodicity' of his thought, dividing the years in which he had known the Tsar into periods of conflicting enthusiasms. In 1805, when he had first met Alexander, the Tsar had been in the throes of a liberal phase, then with the rapprochement with Napoleon in 1807 he had undergone a period of conservatism before responding to the inflamed spirit of 1813 and moving towards a phase of philanthropy and liberalism again. This too had waned and by 1818 he was becoming once more the champion of a conservative order. Altogether then this was a man of mercurial temperament.

Alexander's interest in European stability was patently obvious. His concept of a peaceful universe, founded on the principles of Christian cooperation, had been propagated in the Holy Alliance. What concerned Metternich was Alexander's approach to stability, for whereas Metternich saw a conservative social order as the essential pre-condition for stability, Alexander was not so certain. At his right hand was his chief minister, the Greek nobleman Capo d'Istria, who was an opponent of Metternich's repressive conservatism and urged that stability would be better ensured by a policy of compromise – the solution to social revolution was mediation rather than repression. Whereas concession seemed to Metternich the ultimate folly and weakness, to Alexander, the author of the original and ambiguous script of the Holy Alliance, it might seem constructive. Thus the willingness of Alexander to intervene in Europe was not altogether welcome, for, quite apart from strategic reservations about allowing Russia to play a military role in Europe, Metternich was far from sure that Russian intervention would contribute to the kind of European order he was looking for.

Prussia and France

Of Prussia, the remaining Power in the Quadruple Alliance, Metternich was fairly confident, for Frederick William had enough on his mind as he strove to secure the loyalty and obedience of his new dominions, without running the risk of alienating Austria. But Prussian solidarity was not enough. If Metternich's ideal was Great Power solidarity his tolerable minimum must involve a working majority. If he could not hold Britain, whose insular location made her something of a special case, he must retain the loyalty of Russia, for without it there would be no kind of moral consensus on the need for order and in the consequent confusion France might just as well choose to go the irresponsible way of Russia as the sounder and more conservative way of Austria and Prussia. Metternich was soon uneasy about the trend of events in Bourbon France, as he saw Talleyrand replaced by the Duc de Richelieu, an émigré who had spent the Napoleonic period in the service of the Tsar as Governor of Odessa, and as he watched with suspicion the activities of Pozzo di Borgo, the Tsar's scheming ambassador in Paris.

Metternich's tactics

Metternich proved infinitely resourceful in his attempts to hold the Powers to his interpretation of the alliance during the years following 1815. He used his limited armoury to maximum effect. To Castlereagh he urged the broadest possible interpretation of the Quadruple Alliance, whilst the British Cabinet stood firmly on the narrowest possible interpretation, namely, that the alliance pledged them to action only in the event of an assault on the territorial settlement agreed in the Second Treaty of Paris or in

Legend:

Russia in 1771

Russian gains 1772–1815

In the process of expansion, Russia at war with:

Turkey { 1768–74
1787–92
1806–12 }

France { 1798–1800
1805–07
1812–15 }

Persia 1804–13
Sweden 1808–09

THE RUSSIAN MENACE: RUSSIAN TERRITORIAL ACQUISITIONS
1772–1815

the event of a further attempt by Napoleon to seize power. On
the other hand he tended to adopt the British attitude to the
terms of the alliance, when expounding it to Alexander, for
whilst he wanted to commit Britain further he wanted to re-
strict the scope of Alexander's aspirations. Metternich was prepared in fact to use any material that he could lay his hands on
to curb Alexander and he followed up his dual interpretation of
the terms of the Quadruple Alliance by making good use of the
Holy Alliance, a document for which he had little genuine sympathy but which he proceeded to manipulate to his own advantage. Whereas the British approach to Europe was hard headed
and essentially political, Alexander's had strong moral overtones.
He yearned to dominate the new ethos, to personify the new
Europe. There was about him the fervour of the evangelist.
Sensing this, Metternich made it a cardinal point of policy to
communicate with Alexander in the semi-mystical terms that he
favoured and inch by inch Metternich set out to convince the
Tsar that the crusade that he had launched with the Holy Alliance was in fact the very conservative crusade that Metternich
himself was conducting from a more practical standpoint. If the
'enthusiasm' of the Tsar could be harnessed to Metternich's
cause, then the eccentricities of British policy would be less
alarming. But it was to be a lengthy struggle and an unnerving
one, for the European convulsions of the early twenties were to
place a severe strain on Metternich and the principles that he
proclaimed, as the Powers worked out their priorities in practice.

[12] THE CONGRESS SYSTEM 1818–22

Fortunately, from Metternich's point of view, there was afoot in
Europe after the Napoleonic wars a very strong consciousness of
the need to find new and effective ways of preserving peace and,
what was more, the idea of further cooperation between the
Powers was firmly embedded in the treaty structure of 1815.

The vision of a twenty year solidarity against French aggression, which had found practical expression in the Treaty of Chaumont, had led on to the idea of periodic conferences according to the terms of the Quadruple Alliance. Peace was to be ensured, it was hoped, by a system of collective security. Differences were to be discussed round the conference table, mutual assistance given where necessary and majority decisions adhered to. These were the ideas enshrined in the so-called 'Congress System'.

The idea of regular Great Power Congresses to discuss matters of common import suited Metternich admirably. Not only would they serve as a majestic demonstration of Great Power solidarity, or so he hoped, but they would also give scope for his own particular skills in the handling of men. Metternich was at his best when dealing with people on a personal basis. The lesser men he could usually outmanoeuvre, as he had shown in his handling of Lord Aberdeen in late 1813, and when confronted with tougher opposition he could mobilise a formidable armoury of charm and resourcefulness, as he was to demonstrate time and again in his dealings with Alexander over these years. The prime danger, of course, was that if the Congresses could serve as an impressive show-case for unity, they could equally well prove a disastrous demonstration of disaffection and distrust. Once again Metternich was back to the central problem of how to sustain the loyalty of the Powers to the essence of the Vienna Settlement, as he interpreted it.

The Congress of Aix-la-Chapelle

The delicacy of the task was made all too clear at the first post-war Congress, which was held at Aix-la-Chapelle in the autumn of 1818. The raison d'être of this Congress was the restoration of France to Great Power status; she was to be relieved of the burden of what was left of the indemnity and the army of occupation was to be withdrawn. All four Powers could see the need for these moves and the business was efficiently and briskly completed, France being introduced into the councils of the Great Powers and the Quadruple Alliance being secretly reaffirmed by the Four as a continuing security against further French aggression. As business proceeded so smoothly, Metternich wrote to his wife in confident vein: 'I have never seen a prettier little Congress: this one will produce no bad blood in me, I promise you'.

Castlereagh too was expansive, as he reported back to London: 'placed as the Cabinets now are side by side to each other, misconceptions have been immediately obviated and a divergence of opinion is likely to be avoided'. However, it was not to be for on 8 October, three days after Metternich's letter, the Tsar produced a memorandum which was to emphasise the fundamental division within the alliance. The memorandum urged the Powers to accept the broadest possible interpretation of the post-war treaty structure, to bind themselves in an *alliance solidaire* against domestic revolt, wherever it might occur, and to give a reciprocal guarantee that they would in no way seek to extend or alter the territorial structure of Vienna. In other words, the Tsar was demanding the most extensive commitment to intervention on the conservative principle.

It was clear, of course, that the British Cabinet would never accept such an interpretation of its obligations to the cause of European stability. Indeed recent events had further emphasised the limited nature of Britain's view of her continental role, for she had urged that the Congress of Aix-la-Chapelle be summoned not on the authority of Article VI of the Quadruple Alliance, which implied a broad European concern, but on that of Article V of the Peace of Paris, which had provided for an allied meeting three years hence from the date of signing to review the situation in France. The British approach to continental responsibility was thus narrowed to the minimum. But Metternich too was uneasy about the Tsar's memorandum. It was not, of course, that he disliked its ultra conservative flavour, but he was uneasy about its undertones, for the memorandum went on to suggest that once stability had been assured then greater liberties could safely be granted to the peoples. Alexander was clearly in an ambiguous mood and Metternich was far from eager to give him carte-blanche to march his armies across Europe in a series of interventionist crusades.

So torn was Metternich between the desire to have at his disposal the means of repression and the fear of undue Russian influence in the west that he had even supported the British demand that the Congress be summoned on the authority of the Peace of Paris, for only by narrowing the scope of the Congress could he hope to control the Tsar. Metternich was now in the predicament that he most feared, for a situation looked to be developing where he, the champion of corporate solidarity, would have to make a choice between Britain and Russia. It was a heavy prospect, for in Castlereagh he had his most reliable sympathiser, but in Alexander he saw his greatest danger. Which would be the better policy, to confirm a friendship or to woo the enemy?

In fact the disaster of an open rift was avoided at Aix-la-Chapelle, for the Tsar succumbed to a mixture of persuasion (Metternich) and intransigence (Castlereagh) and withdrew the proposal for the alliance solidaire, but it was clear that the fundamental differences between the approach of the continental Powers to intervention and that of Britain could not be glossed over for much longer. With France now reinstated in the Great Power bloc British opinion on the whole regarded its continental commitment as completed and there was little that the unfortunate Castlereagh, with his lonely vision of regular congress diplomacy, could do to bring Britain further into Europe. Before long a minor crisis would occur, one of the Powers would call for joint action and the British position would be starkly exposed.

Reluctant though he was to commit himself, Metternich really had little choice. Russia was a much more direct threat than Britain and whereas the withdrawal of Britain from the alliance would have an essentially negative effect, the withdrawal of Russia might lead to a positive challenge to the existing balance. Metternich could better afford to lose Britain than Russia, the more so in that he had the comforting knowledge that while Castlereagh remained at the Foreign Office, however detached Britain might appear, the instincts of her Foreign Minister would be generous towards the Austrian quest for peace and stability rather than the reverse. And so, as the decade of the twenties opened, Metternich adjusted his sights to realities, faced up to the fragility of the British relationship with Europe and concentrated his full energies on the impressionable mind of Alexander.

The Congress of Troppau

The rift in the allied ranks was made explicit when two revolts, one in Spain starting in January 1820 and the other in Naples starting in July, gave the Tsar the opportunity to press for a further Congress. Since that Congress would clearly be concerned with intervention and since both revolts were in part concerned to substitute constitutional rule for autocracy, Britain was not to be counted upon. Metternich, reluctant though he was to allow Alexander scope for his interventionist fervour, could see no way round the summoning of a Congress and the consequent exposure of the allied divisions, for he was determined that intervention in Naples must have a corporate sanction lest it be construed as an act of purely selfish Austrian motivation. Having failed to satisfy the Tsar with the suggestion of a Conference of Ministers in Vienna, which might have avoided a public display of disunity, Metternich agreed to the meeting of a Congress at Troppau on 20 October. To this the Powers east of the Rhine came fully represented, while Britain and France sent only observers.

At this congress Metternich set himself the task of mastering Alexander, for he must be assured that Alexander's current enthusiasm for intervention would be directed towards the maintenance of conservative principles and would not become a channel for the implementation of Capo d'Istria's dangerous ideas. As Metternich rightly saw it, he and Capo d'Istria were involved in a crucial struggle for the mastery of the mind of the Tsar. If Metternich lost the battle, his concept of the European order was lost too, for Capo d'Istria's ideas were full of folly, as Metternich saw it.

His principles are utterly democratic. He lives only for his principles and the execution thereof. A great propensity for false philosophy, confusion of thought, pursuit of his favourite studies, these are the outstanding shades of his democracy. He is at once a great ideologist, guardian of democracy, reformer of Poland, protector of the enfranchisement of the Greeks and the civilisation of Bessarabia. . . . I confess that it would not take as much to drive me mad.

To Metternich's great relief he found the Tsar repentant of his early liberalism and by no means the slave of his chief minister's enthusiasms, if his record of the Tsar's remarks at their first meeting on 21 October is to be believed: 'From the year 1813 to 1820 is seven years and these seven years are like a century to me. In the year 1820 I will at no price do what I did in the year 1813. You are not altered, but I am. You have nothing to regret, but I have'. Metternich still had a good chance of saving the Tsar from the irresponsibility of Capo d'Istria, it seemed.

Meanwhile, the debate on the Naples rebellion went much as Metternich had expected. Austria, Russia and Prussia issued a preliminary protocol on 19 November, in which they claimed the right to intervene in domestic revolution, where such unrest constituted a threat to neighbouring states. It was further agreed that the King of Naples should be invited to meet the representatives of the Powers to discuss the Neapolitan situation. In other words, it was a fair assumption that the King would request the very intervention that the Eastern Powers wished to carry through. The response of the British Cabinet was firm. In a circular of 19 January 1821 they declined to join in a scheme of intervention which they believed to constitute unjustifiable interference in the domestic affairs of Naples and to have no authority in the treaty structure of 1815. The division between Britain and the Eastern Powers was now explicit.

The Congress of Laibach

Metternich was therefore all the more in need of a firm understanding with Alexander, for the British withdrawal left him no alternative option. He thus returned to the battle with redoubled vigour when the Eastern Powers reassembled at Laibach, in January 1821, to discuss the Neapolitan situation with

King Ferdinand. The importance that Metternich attached to his conversations with Alexander at this time can be clearly seen in his memoirs, which are full of references to them; part boastful, part sentimental and part naïve, these references reflect intense concern. One gets the impression that what Metternich is really trying to do is to convince himself that he is succeeding in his vital mission.

7 February: this evening I spent three hours with the Emperor Alexander. I cannot rightly describe the impression which I appeared to make on him. My words sounded like a voice from the other world. The inward feeling of the Emperor has, moreover, altered considerably and to this I believe I have much contributed.

Then again on 9 May,

today I had a long conversation with the Emperor Alexander. I venture to say that there is no one in the world clever and intelligent enough to add anything to what was actually spoken between me and the Emperor. If ever anyone turned from black to white, he has.

There are lighter touches here and there, but even then the urgency of the focal problems is not forgotten for long: 'if we drink tea alone together, we agree very well ... ah! if that aromatic beverage could only set Capo d'Istria's head a little right. Good heavens, what a cargo of tea would I import from China'. And then, as the congress drew to a close, Metternich followed up the conversations with a lengthy written exhortation to the Tsar, as a tangible reminder of the accord they had struck and in the hope that he would remain true to his better self, when tucked away at St Petersburg in the company of the pernicious Capo d'Istria. The exhortation ended on a suitably evocative note:

in one word, Sire, let us be conservative; let us walk steadily and firmly on well-known paths: let us not deviate from those lines in word or deed: we shall thus be strong and shall come at last to a time when improvements may be made with as much chance of success as now there is certainty of failure.

It is small wonder that Metternich's tone here took on an almost religious quality, for the rebellion in Naples was followed in 1821 by a rising in Piedmont and a series of Greek risings against Turkish rule. While the Neapolitan rising was effectively quelled by an Austrian force, after due consultation with the King of Naples, and the Piedmontese situation was stabilised by a further Austrian victory and by the threat implicit in the mobilisation of 100 000 Russian troops to assist the Austrians, the Greek problem looked extremely dangerous. Russian expansion at the expense of the Ottoman Empire was a traditional policy and friction over treaty rights was incessant. There were all sorts of ways in which Alexander might be tempted to seize this opportunity for a further assault on the Turks. First and foremost there were the religious overtones of the contest; would Alexander feel drawn to the cause of the Christian Greeks against the infidel Turks, as Baroness von Krüdener urged? As reports of appalling atrocities came in, this seemed more and more a danger, not least when the Patriarch of Constantinople was strung up from the doors of his own cathedral with a number of his bishops on Easter Sunday, 1821. Then again Capo d'Istria was much in favour of some form of Greek independence and Ypsilanti, one of the early leaders of the revolt and an officer in the Russian army, was a former favourite of Alexander. Was all Metternich's good work in bringing the conservative best out in Alexander to be thrown to the winds in a Russian crusade which, if successful, would bring Russian influence yet further West?

Once again Metternich took up the challenge. His line now was to play on Alexander's vanity. The anti-Turkish movement he depicted as the latest offshoot of the revolutionary movement in Europe, against which the Tsar had so bravely and successfully set his face in the recent congresses. In effect he was asking Alexander to sacrifice his territorial ambitions in the south to the better projection of his wise and benevolent image in the West. Metternich's line of approach was clearly reflected in a letter from the Emperor Francis to the Tsar, written in August 1821:

the evil we have to combat is situated in Europe, rather than in Turkey ... in order to shed any illusion about the real nature of their aims, it is only necessary to look at those who now wax so enthusiastic about the so-called christian interests ... they are the very people who do not believe in any God and respect neither his laws nor those of man. ... In the unity of the allied courts resides the last hope to avert the threatening evil.

To this psychological line of approach Metternich added practical encouragement. He underlined the fact that as far as Austria was concerned there were two distinct issues involved in the Greek risings. There was a dispute in the Danube Principalities of Moldavia and Wallachia over the exact stipulations of the 1812 Treaty of Bucharest between Russia and the Porte and then there was the infinitely larger issue of the claim of the Greeks of the Morea to independence. In a letter of 28 January 1822 Metternich made it quite clear that Austria would give full support to Russian claims over treaty violations, but that the larger, indeed the revolutionary issue of Greek independence should go before an allied congress.

In this prolonged contest for Alexander's renunciation of expansion, Metternich had two advantages. The first was that the possibility of Russian expansion into the Mediterranean was profoundly disturbing to Britain. Thus Castlereagh, who had not so long ago harangued the Eastern Powers for their pursuit of policies of precaution, was now to be found writing in strong terms to the Tsar, urging him to stand firm against this further manifestation of the revolutionary spirit!

This British pressure tied up with Metternich's other advantage, which was the Tsar's own character. Metternich had gambled from the start on his belief that the Tsar so valued his European image that he would not lightly surrender it. The prospect of isolation, if he did now pursue an expansionist policy, was not one that Alexander relished and the temporary restoration of solidarity between Britain and Austria served as a powerful reminder of the loneliness that might follow from a rejection of western opinion. Temperamentally more in tune with Metternich than with Capo d'Istria by now, the Tsar allowed himself to be gently led away from the aggressive opportunity that had presented itself and when in May 1822 the Sultan was prevailed upon to make a generous offer Alexander accepted it unquestioningly.

The larger problem of Greek independence was reserved for the Congress of Verona but there can be no more convincing demonstration of the extent of Metternich's success by cool and dogged perseverance than the fact that in June 1822 Capo d'Istria went on indefinite leave to Switzerland. In fact he never regained power in Russia and he was ultimately assassinated in 1831, as he strove to coordinate the newly independent Greece – an apt case of the punishment fitting the crime from Metternich's point of view perhaps.

The Congress of Verona

As the tension momentarily slackened with Alexander's rejection of a policy of unilateral action against the Turk, attention shifted to the forthcoming Congress at Verona. The revival of positive British action over the Greek issue seemed to offer some hope that an effective allied solidarity might now be recovered, but the hope proved short-lived, for in August 1822 Castlereagh committed suicide and his successor, Canning, was to personify all that Metternich most regretted in Britain's self-centred attitude towards Europe. If Castlereagh had had strict reservations about the extent of British commitment in Europe, Canning was even more withdrawn. For Canning, unlike Castlereagh, was a man of the people. Whereas Castlereagh registered the insularity of popular opinion but tried to bypass it as far as possible, Canning made positive capital out of it, reflecting and indeed magnifying that insularity. This is not to say that he was not ready to assist in a European emergency that really threatened British interests, but rather that he was not prepared to disguise the fact that his interests were primarily British rather than European. Thus Metternich's arguments for a European consciousness transcending selfish and particular interests would carry little weight with him.

Metternich was fully aware of the significance of Castlereagh's death. On 25 August he wrote in gloom:

it is one of the worst catastrophes that could have befallen me. He was devoted to me heart and soul, not only from a personal attachment, but also from conviction. Many matters which would have been easy with him are going to need fresh study and renewed effort with his successor, whoever he may be ... for the moment I am left on my own and am thrown back on my own resources.

Of Canning, with his disregard for the laws of natural evolution, Metternich was soon to draw an unfavourable picture: 'to advance by bounds, to attack things for no other reason than to get oneself talked about, to launch oneself passionately down unknown paths and to get out of breath in the process, that is not governing'. In similar vein was Metternich's epitaph on Canning, after his sudden and unexpected death in 1827:

Mr Canning undertook a great deal, but finished nothing. He knocked down and undermined a great deal, but he built nothing. His ministry [Canning became Prime Minister in April 1827], which lasted only three months, will occupy a place in the annals of history similar to that of another famous Hundred Days. Both of these periods resemble an irruption, they present a picture of avalanches blotting out everything in their path that is not actually destroyed. But that which has only been submerged will not take long to come through again. . . . I was perhaps less struck by his sudden death than most people, because I knew of the danger that threatened him. It was not only his body that was attacked, but even his mind. Too much activity on the part of the cogs had broken the machine.

So sure was Metternich of the right-mindedness of his own conservative approach. (See his views on Széchenyi, Part V, pp. 144–5.)

Britain was in fact represented at Verona by Wellington, not Canning, but there could be little doubt that the British mood would be uncooperative if Alexander resumed his interventionist line of approach, as he was almost certain to do, having just denied himself the opportunity for action against Turkey. Sure enough the Tsar arrived urging corporate intervention not in Greece, an issue which the Verona Congress decided that the Turks should settle for themselves, but in Spain, where an attempt to overthrow the Constitutionalists on behalf of the King had just failed, to Alexander's chagrin. This issue split the alliance again, just as the issue of corporate intervention had split it at Troppau. Once more Metternich was forced to recognise that the hope of recovering British solidarity was illusory and that the best he could hope for was a fair degree of unanimity amongst the four continental Powers.

The issue of Spain was more explosive than that of Naples had been. Over the Italian revolts Britain had not been prepared to intervene herself, but had recognised Austria's right to do so. Over Spain Britain was adamantly opposed to intervention of any kind. It was not so much her sympathy for the constitutionalists in Spain that fired her (liberal sympathies alone have rarely provoked a strong British stand in foreign policy) as the fact that she had no desire to see a successful intervention in Spain, which might have repercussions in the Spanish American Empire, which was in the process of achieving its independence. Certainly she had no desire to see Spain recover control in Spanish America and then farm out trading privileges there to the Powers who had assisted her in that recovery. The situation thus became extremely tense when the French showed a marked enthusiasm to take up the Russian plan for intervention, for of all the Powers France was the one best suited to expansion as a maritime trading Power, and she had an additional incentive in that there was the Bourbon family relationship to assist in a closer understanding between Paris and Madrid.

Metternich was in an awkward spot. He had no desire to see Russian troops in Europe again, nor did he relish the renewed signs of aggressive vitality in France, but since he could clearly not count on England for any kind of consistent support he must make a gesture towards Alexander. Accordingly Austria and Prussia agreed to withdraw their ambassadors from Madrid if France should do so, but Metternich continued to stress the desirability of a peaceful solution. Chateaubriand, the French Foreign Minister, eventually decided to risk intervention on the grounds that nobody would do anything positive to prevent it and the French duly restored Ferdinand in the summer of 1823.

Once again Metternich was made acutely conscious of the fact that he could rely with more safety on the caution of the Powers east of the Rhine than those west of it. Accordingly during the

Verona Congress he wrote yet another memorandum to Alexander, reminding him of the need for solidarity and urging yet greater vigilance against the revolutionary peril:

never has the world shown examples of union and solidarity in great political bodies such as those given by Russia, Austria and Prussia in the course of the last few years. By separating carefully the concerns of self-preservation from ordinary politics, and by subordinating all individual interests to the common and general interest, the monarchs have found the true means of maintaining their holy union and accomplishing the enormous good which they have achieved ... as this solidarity exists between the three northern governments, it is necessary to bring the French government to join it as much as possible.

This really was Metternich's policy as it evolved in practice and in the light of experience. Fondly though he might continue to nourish the dream of five-Power solidarity, the post-war years had taught him that the more practical possibility was a compromise solution. Britain could never be relied upon consistently: her island prejudices and her fluctuating parliamentary system were insuperable. France was a more possible convert, though one to be watched with care for her past gave scant reason for confidence. The hard core, on which the maintenance of a conservative system depended, was the Eastern bloc and in many ways the success or failure of Metternich's policies was to depend right through to his fall on his ability to sustain Russian loyalty. The Congress System was dead in practice, for Britain would not undertake such a commitment. The task now was to maintain the solidarity of the continental Powers and in particular that of the eastern trio.

[13] THE GREEK WAR

If Metternich had been forced to abandon the rosy vision of five-Power solidarity on conservative principles in 1822, he was shortly to despair of any kind of right-minded solidarity whatso-

ever, for the mid-twenties witnessed the triumph of those selfish
and particular interests which Metternich had hoped to subordinate to the general. The death of Castlereagh and the advent
of Canning had initiated the new phase, one which was further
consolidated by the death of Alexander in December 1825 and
the accession of his brother Nicholas. With Britain and Russia
both less attentive to Metternich's views, it was no longer possible to count even on a conservative majority in the balance of
the five Powers, let alone a conservative unanimity.

The central issue of the period was the Greek war, which had
started almost unnoticed in 1821 and which had gathered dangerous momentum before anybody came to take it very seriously.
From Metternich's point of view, it was a major tragedy that
the insurrection was not firmly repressed at the outset. Had the
Porte acted firmly, whilst the solidarity of the Powers was still
more or less intact, then the disastrous sequence of events in the
later twenties might well have been averted. Unfortunately,
however, the Porte did little or nothing about the revolt at first
and by the time that it did decide on firmer steps the Greek
insurrection had succeeded in gaining a good deal of sympathy
in Europe, where the sentimental Phil-hellenist movement provided enthusiastic and emotional backing for a cause which was
somewhat misleadingly depicted as a struggle for the virtues and
values of the classical tradition. Backed in this way, the Greeks
were in no mood to stand down, when the Turks at last took a
determined interest in the rebellion. The result was a deadlock, in
which neither side was prepared to think in terms of concession.

Metternich's attitude to the Greek struggle was generally in
keeping with his much-vaunted principles. Turkey was a legitimate Power and the Greeks were not. As he wrote to Lebzeltern,
his ambassador in St Petersburg, 'whatever may be the moral
condition of the Porte, it has for the Courts the value of a regular
Power. The Revolution is of an entirely different character'. It
might nonetheless be, as Metternich himself was reluctantly
driven to admit in 1825, that in order to survive the Porte would
have to make concessions to the Greeks. In the same letter to
Lebzeltern he wrote

in fact the thing to be done is to announce to the Porte that, in case of a peremptory refusal of concessions considered indispensable, the Powers decided at all costs to end the present troubles, see the necessity of admitting the independence of the Morea and the islands, if the Porte does not make this resolution unnecessary by wise and efficacious measures, fitted to put an end to a state of things incompatible for the peace and well-being of Europe.

But, whatever the solution, Metternich was adamant that the Powers should deal with the Porte as its friends and not as its opponents and that only by solidarity behind the Porte's legitimacy could the anarchic possibilities of a scramble for power at the Porte's expense be avoided.

Russia in conflict with the Porte

Such a line would not be easily sustained, for there were subversive influences at work, which were less sensitive than Metternich to the claims of legitimacy. Russia was still in a state of constant conflict with the Porte, despite the apparently successful easing of tension in 1822. In particular she contested the Turkish right to station troops in the Principalities of Moldavia and Wallachia and she bitterly resented Turkish restrictions on her maritime freedom in the Black Sea. It was all too clear that if these differences were not cleared up, then Russia would be the more likely to take up the cause of the Greeks in retaliation. Metternich had never ceased to bewail the folly of the Turks in their suspicious hostility to Alexander and his comments on the maritime issue were typical of his broad conviction that the Porte was cutting its own throat (and subjecting European peace to an intolerable strain in the process!):

the Ottoman Government appears to me to be following the line of conduct too often followed by private individuals in a state of bankruptcy. Knowing no longer how to retain possession of their fortune, they take to speculations which, even if they succeeded, could not save them from ruin. It is a calculation of this kind which makes the Divan fix its hopes on the navigation of the Turks, a navigation which in the days of the empire's prosperity did not exist, and which certainly cannot be created in a time of disaster.

While Alexander lived, Metternich was able to maintain his crucial point that while Russia's treaty disputes with the Porte were her own affair, the Greek issue was a matter for the Powers in concert; but to Nicholas this distinction was to seem less binding.

Closely allied to Russia in Metternich's thinking was France. Even in the moment of victory in 1814 Metternich had feared an understanding between Russia and France that would run counter to his own thinking and he had never ceased to view with distaste the machinations of Pozzo di Borgo, the Tsar's ambassador in Paris. The main reason for Metternich's concern was that he still regarded France with suspicion and feared that if given a lead she would not be slow to abandon the restrictions of the conservative alliance. The Power most likely to give that lead was surely Russia, whose aggressive instincts had so nearly ruined the Vienna negotiations, for Britain was firmly opposed to French expansion and Prussia was more or less safely in line with Austria. Thus, if Metternich were to lose his hold on Russia he would not be unduly surprised to find France adopting an independent line too, for her yearning for gloire had already been made clear in her determined approach to the issue of Spanish intervention.

British sympathy for the Greek cause

Then there was Britain. The independence of British thinking was something that Metternich had reluctantly accepted. As far back as March 1823 the British had recognised the Greeks as belligerents, but this was not so much a declaration of faith in the rebellion as a measure to protect shipping in waters that were dominated by Greeks rather than Turks. As time went on, however, the British Government became increasingly sympathetic to the Greek cause. Canning tended to believe that movements for independence, which could prove their ability to survive under pressure, should be accepted, unless they constituted a major threat to fundamental British interests. Thus the British had recognised the independence of the Spanish American Colonies, whilst Metternich and his supporters had insisted upon opposing it, and logically enough it was to Britain that the Greek rebels turned for protection in June 1825, when the Turkish Sultan unleashed on the Morea the troops of his Egyptian vassal, Mehemet Ali.

Alexander's death was thus particularly ill-timed as far as Metternich was concerned. Just as the Greek crisis looked to be boiling up to a decisive phase, he lost the partial security of having in Russia a ruler over whom he had some influence and almost before he could get acclimatised to the new situation the worst had happened. Canning, eager to bring the Mediterranean crisis to a satisfactory conclusion, had taken over Metternich's role as custodian of the Tsar. With masterly opportunism he despatched the Duke of Wellington to proffer to Nicholas the compliments of the English king on his accession and also to discuss the Greek issue. Wellington was an ideal choice for his impact on the soldierly Nicholas was considerable and provided Canning with the advantage that he wanted. Canning's motives were complex. He was inclined to secure some gains for the Greeks certainly, but he had no desire to see Russia demolish the Turkish Empire and establish for herself an untrammelled outlet into the Mediterranean. Rather, he hoped that by offering mediation to the Porte in alliance with Russia he would be able to engineer a peaceful solution to the crisis without giving Russia the opportunity to invade the Turkish Empire. This was the purpose of the Protocol of 4 April 1826, which bound Britain and Russia to mediate for Greek independence under Turkish suzerainty.

Essentially peaceable though Canning's motives may have been, his method was anathema to Metternich, who dismissed the protocol of April as 'an abortion which in a few weeks will be disowned by the very people who contrived it'. He was to put his objections more coherently in November 1827: 'the whole affair turns on the words Mediation and Pacification. It did so at the beginning and now it is plainer still. The first word represents the revolutionary principle: the second everlasting right'. For

Metternich there could never be mediation between legitimate authority and revolutionary forces, for this would be to recognise a legitimacy in those revolutionary forces. The only legitimate solution would be one imposed or granted on the initiative of the Porte. The result of this British move could only be to worsen the situation, for the Porte would become more intransigent at this affront to its legitimate rights, whilst the rebels would become more determined as a result of what to their eyes amounted to recognition by Britain and Russia.

The Treaty of London

If Metternich expected a landslide to follow this rejection of sound principles, he was not disappointed. Despite a settlement of her grievances in the Danube Principalities by the Treaty of Akkerman (October 1826), Russia proved determined to pursue her interest in the Greek issue too. Furthermore, the programme of mediation found additional support when, in July 1827, France joined Britain and Russia in the Treaty of London, which undertook to enforce an armistice between the Greeks and the Turks, if they would not accept one voluntarily. And so, for the first time, Metternich found himself positively outnumbered in the counsels of the Great Powers. As he stood powerless on the sidelines, it looked very much as though Europe was to be hurled back into a period of revolutionary conflict, with the Powers competing for spoils, as the Ottoman Empire finally fell apart. The unexpected death of Canning on 8 August 1827 deprived the Triple Alliance both of its creator and of its bridle and in the confusion that followed the combined Turkish and Egyptian fleets were annihilated at Navarino in October. What had started in Canning's mind as a move to exact some sense from the Porte by the mere threat of force had now degenerated into actual war. In 1828 a French expedition entered the Morea and Russian forces began operations in Moldavia and Wallachia plus a march on Constantinople. It began to look very much as though Russia was replacing France as the major revolutionary threat to European stability. Metternich protested in a letter of March 1828:

the new Russian manifestoes are modelled on those of the French
Empire; it is not only the fundamental idea which is identical, but
the manner of putting it, of disguising it, of making it fluent – all
recalls their style.

As considerations of equilibrium faded into the background,
Metternich gloomily reviewed the inadequacy of Habsburg resources. Unable to impose an equilibrium on Europe by force,
even if he had wished to do so, Metternich was dependent on
maintaining a moral consensus in its favour. This he had failed
to do and the stubbornness of the Porte had deprived him of his
one last hope – that limited concessions by the Sultan would be
forthcoming in time to forestall the outbreak of war. For Metternich even to think in terms of concession as a solution was un-
characteristic and his agony of mind is clearly to be seen in his
reluctant efforts to tailor his principles to the demands of the
current situation. His memorandum of March 1828, as Russia
was about to start military operations, had none of the confident
ring of earlier pronouncements:

it is a fact that revolutions the most culpable in their origin have
sometimes ended triumphantly [such a confession would have been
impossible in 1820!], and that when this has come to pass the enlightened and correct governments have been obliged to come to
terms with the most undoubted usurpation. If, then, the peace of
Europe is attached to the pacification of the Levant, and if the independence of part of Greece, with all the inconveniences and dangers
it will entail, is the unavoidable condition of this pacification, it is
no longer possible to hesitate.

A similar concern to make the best of a bad job can be seen in a
letter to Esterhazy, also written in March 1828: 'the choice no
longer exists between what we qualify as good and evil. The good
having been rendered impossible, we have only to deal with the
evil, and to do all in our power to lessen its consequences'. Gone
is Metternich's original insistence on the sanctity of the territorial structure of Vienna. In its place we find a desperate groping
for a means to stop Russia and to preserve as much of the Ottoman Empire as is possible in the circumstances, for Metternich
is really lost in a context where neither side regards the equili-

brium as the major issue and where reference to principles is meaningless. He had really summed up his own dilemma in a survey of the situation, made as early as May 1823: 'the Greek insurrection is, so to speak, entirely beyond the domain of diplomacy; it has become a question of fact, a problem which Providence alone in the depth of its wisdom can resolve'. Metternich certainly could not resolve a struggle in which neither of the principal participants, Russia and Turkey, really spoke his own language.

The Treaty of Adrianople

In a way Providence did play a role in the struggle, for Europe certainly emerged from it less disastrously than Metternich had expected. Mainly as a result of the exhaustion of the Russian armies, who found the Turks more difficult than they had anticipated, a moderate peace was imposed in September 1829 by the Treaty of Adrianople. The Russians remained in occupation of the Danube Principalities, pending the payment of an indemnity of fifteen million ducats. Meanwhile, a carefully mapped Greek State was granted autonomy and eventually acquired an hereditary monarchy in 1832, all in accordance with the terms of the London Protocol, which was signed by Russia, France and Britain in March 1829. So the just equilibrium was not grossly distorted to suit Russian ends.

Nonetheless, Metternich had learned a tough lesson. His faith in his own principles as the key to European repose was unshaken, but he was increasingly certain that those principles would carry weight only if Austria was strong enough to back them by the threat of force. Reviewing the significance of the Treaty of Adrianople in October 1829, he wrote to the Emperor:

with regret we must confess that the Eastern Question would neither have been so seriously discussed, nor have had such unfortunate results, if Austria had been in a different position from that in which she now finds herself after the reductions of the past thirteen years ... the belief in the entire exhaustion of our strength, even if founded less on reality than on general prejudice, has certainly not been with-

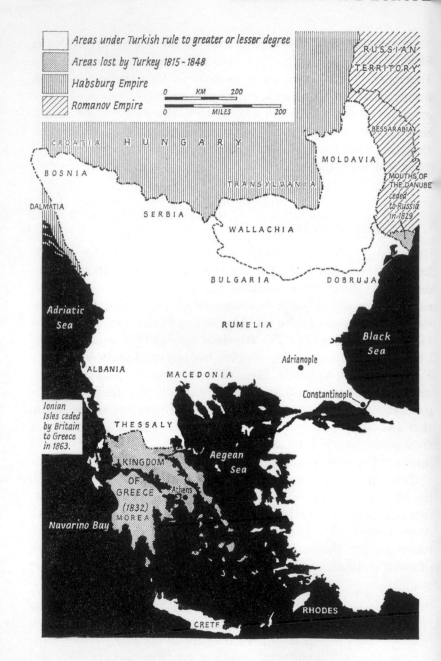

Legend:
- Areas under Turkish rule to greater or lesser degree
- Areas lost by Turkey 1815-1848
- Habsburg Empire
- Romanov Empire

0 ___ KM ___ 200
0 ___ MILES ___ 200

RUSSIAN TERRITORY

CROATIA HUNGARY

BOSNIA

DALMATIA

SERBIA

TRANSYLVANIA

MOLDAVIA

BESSARABIA

MOUTHS OF
THE DANUBE
ceded
to Russia
in 1829

WALLACHIA

BULGARIA

DOBRUJA

Adriatic
Sea

RUMELIA

Black
Sea

Adrianople

ALBANIA

MACEDONIA

Constantinople

Ionian
Isles ceded
by Britain
to Greece
in 1863.

THESSALY

Aegean
Sea

KINGDOM
OF
GREECE
(1832)
MOREA

Athens

Navarino Bay

RHODES

CRETE

THE OTTOMAN EMPIRE IN EUROPE 1815–48

out the most troublesome influence on the course of events over the
past eight years.

Urging the Emperor on to a programme of vigorous military and
financial reform, Metternich looked on to the years ahead in a
grimly practical frame of mind. His helplessness in recent events
had taught him that his diplomatic skills needed firmer backing
than had recently been available.

[14] THE REVOLUTIONS OF 1830

Metternich's conviction that nothing short of Great Power solidarity would suffice to extinguish the revolutionary virus was
reinforced when, hard on the heels of the divided approach to
the problem of Greece, there followed a series of revolutions in
1830. The overthrow of the Bourbon regime in France, followed
by a successful revolution in Belgium and abortive revolts in
Poland and Italy, left Metternich pensive and unsure of himself.
The buoyant optimism of 1815 had given way to a sneaking
pessimism; as he wrote to Nesselrode, 'my most secret thought is
that the old Europe has come to the beginning of the end ...
from another point of view the new Europe is not yet begun;
between the beginning and the end there lies chaos'.

It was not that Metternich's fundamental views had changed,
but that whilst revolutionary ideas had taken a further and
dramatic step forward, he could see no hope of the kind of solidarity that was needed if conservatism were to prevail. He could
have no real faith in the new French regime, which was itself the
child of revolution. Whatever Louis Philippe's intentions, he
was hopelessly compromised. As Metternich was to put it later,
in August 1842, 'it is France's misfortune to be ungovernable
and she is in this unhappy position because the debris of social
revolution is poor material for reconstruction and because Louis
XVIII was a miserable architect'.

And if France was not to be counted upon, scarcely more reliable was England, especially during the periods when Palmerston wielded power, for Metternich saw in him the same kind of heady irresponsibility as that which he had already encountered in Canning. It was perhaps as a result of his mounting conviction that real five-power solidarity was an impracticable dream that Metternich at times resorted to more flexible tactics in the thirties, as he had eventually been forced to do over Greece, choosing to surrender his earlier hard-line conservatism and to improvise on a basis of what would be tolerable rather than lay down rigid terms and conditions. Thus when it became clear that the Belgian Revolution of 1830 would have to be recognised, he accommodated himself to this defiance of the Vienna Settlement, concerning himself with the preservation of appearances rather than indulging in a futile defence of outraged principles. 'The great problem will be to prevent the changes which are inevitable from assuming the appearance of concessions extorted by force, and to keep up the appearance at least of sovereign will.'

Response to Metternich's conservatism

Perhaps the most surprising aspect of the period 1830–48 was the relatively successful prolongation of a measure of European repose, despite Metternich's forebodings. In fact, circumstances had taught the Powers a lesson that Metternich's persuasiveness had failed to bring home to them. Ironically enough, the very revolutions that Metternich had tried so hard to avoid had the effect of re-consolidating the Eastern trio in the defence of the status quo and even Britain and France proved surprisingly responsive to conservatism, though perhaps for different reasons – Louis-Philippe in the interests of security and in the hope of gaining recognition from the Eastern monarchs and Britain because of the early reappearance of the Ottoman issue, which was one in which she had a strongly conservative interest anyway. Thus Metternich could fairly comment that,

if the glorious days [the July Revolution in Paris] effected any change in the current affairs, it was that the majority of the Courts, I will even say one and all of them, were induced to assimilate their policies to ours ... unhappily, the dawn had been long in breaking and its light now fell, in every direction, on buildings which had been terribly damaged.

To the conservative solidarity of the Eastern Powers, recon-firmed at Münchengrätz in October 1833 and again at Teplitz in 1835, were added the somewhat erratic approaches of Britain and France, whose counter-alliance of 1834 (with the 'liberal' Queens of Spain and Portugal), proved very much less of a threat to conservatism than Metternich at first feared. Thus Metternich was left with a floating consensus in favour of conservative policies, even though the approach of the Powers fell far short of the determined solidarity that he had originally hoped for.

In his twin concerns for the Vienna equilibrium and for the maintenance of the social order, Metternich got more satisfaction in the former area than in the latter. Actual structural changes between 1830 and 1848 were negligible. The recognition of Greek independence was followed by that of Belgian, when the firm line taken by Britain and France in 1830, coupled with the sub-sequent preoccupation of Austria and Russia with revolt in their own empires, led to five-Power recognition of the partition of the Kingdom of the Netherlands, which had been constructed at Vienna as a barrier against French aggression.

Although disapproving of the domineering attitude of the maritime Powers, Metternich conceded the point that the revised settlement did not constitute a major threat to the equilibrium. Much more dangerous, however, were two attempts by Mehemet Ali to increase his own authority at the expense of that of the Turkish Sultan, who had originally promised him the Morea before being forced to recognise its independence. In both cases the results were satisfactory to Metternich, rather than to the Egyptians. In December 1832 the Turks were defeated by the Egyptians only to be saved by Russia, whose return to the con-servative fold was emphasised by the fact that in the Treaty of Unkiar Skelessi, which she signed with the Porte in July 1833, she exacted no territorial compensation, though she did secure a secret agreement that the Porte would close the Dardanelles in the event of Russia being at war. When in 1839 Mehemet Ali's troops again inflicted crushing defeats on the Turks, who this time had started the war, Metternich was again relieved to find the Great Powers in accord and he was able to consolidate their efforts in a conference of ambassadors, which met at Vienna and produced the Collective Note of 27 July 1839, urging the Sultan to stand firm pending allied intervention. This five-Power solidarity collapsed in February 1840, when Thiers took over the direction of French foreign policy and deserted the allies in favour of a policy of support for Mehemet Ali, but the remaining four stood firm, pledging themselves to armed intervention if necessary by the terms of the Treaty of London, 15 July 1840.

If the dominant role in these later negotiations had passed from Austria to Russia and Britain, the result was again to Metternich's liking, for the fragility of the Franco-British rapprochement had been amply demonstrated and Mehemet Ali was forced to surrender most of his gains to the Sultan in return for the hereditary title to his Egyptian territories. Thus the Mediterranean status quo had been preserved and by decisive corporate action by all but the sickly France, whose short-lived championship of Mehemet Ali had only served to confirm Metternich's reservations about her. For all Palmerston's insularity, he had temporarily restored the solidarity of the four legitimate governments by his approach to the Turkish problem and in July 1841, Thiers having been forced to resign in October 1840, France returned to the fold as well when she joined the other Powers in signing the Straits Convention, which destroyed the secret advantage gained by Russia in the Treaty of Unkiar Skelessi and laid down that the Dardanelles should be permanently closed to warships, save in the event of the Porte herself being at war (in which case her allies might presumably send naval assistance to her).

Liberal unrest

This measure of collaboration between the Great Powers over the maintenance of an equilibrium which represented only a slight modification of the Vienna Settlement was not, however, accompanied by an equally firm approach to the problem of social unrest. Metternich's original concept of a union of legitimate governments against faction, wherever it showed itself, was not to find fulfilment and the revolutionary disease was not to be eliminated, for despite the renewed solidarity of the Eastern Powers on the issue, Britain and France continued to pursue an independent line, thereby allowing the exponents of revolutionary ideas to survive and indeed to prosper.

The most obviously revolutionary area was the Spanish peninsula, for in Spain and in Portugal both Britain and France pledged themselves to the cause of 'liberal' queens against their respective conservative rivals, Don Carlos and Don Miguel, and Metternich had little doubt that it was only through foreign aid that the liberal cause prevailed. As he remarked in September 1834, just after Britain and France had signed a Quadruple Alliance with the Queens' governments, 'the Revolution was perfectly right to select the Iberian Peninsula as the place in which to establish its headquarters. Covered by France and flanked by Britain, it may consider itself placed there under powerful protection'.

The French Government had already given Metternich an uncomfortable reminder of its revolutionary origins, for as early as February 1832 it had dramatically landed an expedition at Ancona in the Papal States with the intention of 'observing' the conduct of the Austrian forces, which had intervened against revolution there. If Austria could intervene on behalf of the Papacy, she would not be allowed to dictate policies to the Pope once stability had been restored, or so the French Government was hinting. The point was made, for the French troops stayed in Ancona for six years, withdrawing only when the Austrians eventually withdrew theirs.

Such direct interference with interventionist policies was rare, but Russian extremes in Poland after the 1830 revolution there, Metternich's own annexation of Cracow in 1846 (p. 148) and his intervention in Italy in 1847 (p. 155), were all bitterly attacked by liberal opinion in the west and it was partly the influence of Palmerston, together with the fact that the radicals' victory

over the conservative Sonderbund was achieved so quickly and
that Habsburg resources were already strained to the limit,
which deterred Metternich from intervention in Switzerland in
1847.

Thus there was no kind of solidarity on the need to suppress
liberal developments and their contagious effects in Europe, even
though there was a measure of willingness to prevent radical
alterations to the territorial balance of Vienna. It is therefore
not surprising that Metternich's fall, when it came in 1848, was
the result of domestic revolt and not of any external assault on
the Habsburg Empire. By his own analysis of the situation back
in 1815, the forces hostile to conservatism could only be subdued
by corporate solidarity. This had not been forthcoming and the
campaign had become a holding action rather than a bid for
outright victory. As he wrote to the Tsar, just after his resignation, 'Europe, Sire, is abandoned to a crisis which is beyond
the scope of a political movement; the crisis is rooted in the
social order. I have seen it coming; I have grappled with it consistently for nearly forty years; it is beyond the power of men to
stop a torrent; all they can do is to staunch its flow.' Unable even
to staunch the flow of revolution in 1848, Metternich was duly
swept away in the torrent.

[15] METTERNICH'S DIPLOMATIC ACHIEVEMENT

In terms of his broad objective, the attainment of full Great
Power commitment to the principles of the Vienna Settlement
as he interpreted them, Metternich was a failure. But it would be
a mistake to probe no further than this, for in terms of his diplomatic objectives Metternich was no more than a partial failure,
if he was even that. Certainly he proved unable to crush revolutionary ideas of territorial aggrandisement or of social revolution
once and for all under the glowering front of legitimate authority,
but in so far as his policies were also designed to gain for the

Habsburg Empire a period of peace, in which to set about a policy of revitalisation, he was remarkably successful, for in the thirty years, 1815–48, Austria was engaged in no major war and suffered no territorial losses. Conservatism had thus scored a measure of success, though admittedly not the total dominance that Metternich believed to be the prerequisite of European reposc.

The predominantly conservative mood of the period was not, of course, simply attributable to Metternich's magical or satanic abilities, much as some tended towards such a view, but his diplomacy was, without doubt, a significant factor. Forced to relinquish at an early stage the idea of five-Power solidarity, Metternich had come to the conclusion that if he could not have unanimity he must at least achieve the next best thing, a majority in the counsels of the five Powers, and it is remarkable to note that only in the years 1827–9 was he really in a minority position.

Regarding England and France as the least reliable of the Powers, he went determinedly in pursuit of Russia and his influence with the Tsars Alexander and Nicholas is really the key to such success as he achieved. Manipulating the fears of both, he succeeded for most of the time in curbing their expansionist tendencies and it is noticeable that the only two occasions on which Metternich's situation became truly desperate were those in which he lost control of Russia. In the Greek War he found himself beset by the vision of Russian successes in the Turkish domains, which would seriously upset both the European equilibrium and Austrian security, and in the forties he witnessed the growth of a Russian understanding with Britain which, although not aggressive in intent, did reflect a tendency on the part of the Tsar to be less immediately responsive to the claims of European conservatism and which did ultimately embarrass the Habsburg Empire in that Russia did not intervene on behalf of order until the 1848 revolutions were well under way. Metternich well knew that the loss of total Russian commitment could not be adequately compensated for by the French drift away from Britain and towards Austria during Guizot's ministry.

Thus Metternich eventually lost the degree of solidarity amongst the Powers that was necessary if the social revolution were to be countered, but he bought time with considerable success. The crucial question for the Empire was whether or not that time could be put to good use internally.

Principal Events, 1815-48

INTERNATIONAL RELATIONS WITHIN EUROPE

Great Power efforts towards stability	*Threats to stability*
1818. September. Congress of Aix-la-Chapelle	
1820.	January. Revolt in Spain
	July. Revolt in Naples
	August. Revolt in Portugal
October. Congress of Troppau	
1821. January. Congress of Laibach	Revolts in Moldavia and
February. Successful Austrian intervention in Naples	Wallachia
	March. Revolt in Piedmont
April. Successful Austrian intervention in Piedmont	Revolt in Greece
1822.	Capo d'Istria's retirement in June offset by Castlereagh's suicide in August and by the succession of Canning
October. Congress of Verona	
1823. April–September. Successful French intervention in Spain	
October. Tsar meets Emperor Francis at Czernowitz and undertakes not to take unilateral action in Greece	
1824. Abortive St Petersburg Conference on the Greek issue	
1825. Further abortive St Petersburg Conferences	February, Ibrahim commences invasion of the Morea
	March. Greek appeal for British protection
	December. Death of Alexander
1826.	March. Russian ultimatum to Turkey re: the Principalities
4 April. Anglo–Russian	Portuguese succession struggle

Protocol
October. Treaty of
Akkerman between Russia
and Turkey and re: the
Principalities

1827. July. Treaty of London

commences. Death of King
John leads to struggle between
Maria and Miguel

August. Death of Canning
October. Battle of Navarino

1828.

French expedition to the
Morea. Russian invasion of the
Principalities and expedition
for Constantinople
Portuguese throne seized by
Don Miguel

1829. March. London Protocol
outlines basis for Greek
independence
September. Treaty of
Adrianople

1830.

July. 'July Revolution' in
Paris
August. Revolution in Belgium

London Conference of the
Powers on Belgian issue
November. First protocol

Revolution in Poland

1831.

Revolts in Parma, Modena
and the Romagna

November. Treaty of London
agrees Belgian independence

1832.

February. French Ancona
expedition
December. Egypto–Turkish
War

1833. July. Russian intervention
on Turkey's behalf leads to
the Treaty of Unkiar
Skelessi
September. Treaty of
Münchengrätz between the
three Eastern Powers

Maria restored with British
help

Ferdinand VII dies and
succession battle commences
between the infant Isabella

		and her uncle, Don Carlos
1834.	Quadruple Alliance of Britain, France and the Queens of Portugal and Spain	
1835.	Müchengrätz understanding confirmed at Teplitz after death of Emperor Francis	
1839.		April. Turkey declares war on Egypt
	27 July. Collective note to the Sultan	
1840.		February. Thiers enters the French Ministry
	15 July. Treaty of London	October. Thiers forced to resign
1841.	July. Straits Convention	
1846.		Austrian annexation of Cracow and a series of riots and constitutional concessions in Italy
		June. Election of Pius IX
1847.	Guizot strongly negotiating for a firmer understanding with Austria, having quarrelled with Britain over Spanish marriages	Defeat of the conservative Sonderbund in Swiss Civil War and the consequent drafting of a progressive constitution for the Swiss cantons
1848.		January. Revolutionary sequence commences in Sicily

PART IV
Metternich and the Empire

[16] THE DOMESTIC PROBLEM

Metternich's diplomacy bought time for the Habsburgs. From 1815 to 1848 no Habsburg territory was lost and Austrian prestige in Europe was generally high. In the long term, however, such diplomatic success was not alone enough. If the Empire were to survive there must be a major effort made to revitalise the ties which held it together. The faith of the Great Powers in the idea of an Austrian Empire, with a vital role to play in central and eastern Europe, must be matched by a new and dynamic loyalty to that same Empire on the part of the provinces which comprised it. Unless this internal triumph could be worked, the diplomatic achievement could be of no more than transitory significance.

It is easy enough to say that what was necessary was for somebody to inject a new logic into the veins of the Habsburg Empire, but it was a daunting picture that confronted the eye of the would-be reformer. The Habsburg possessions were a diverse and sprawling collection, which could under no circumstances be said to form a genuinely 'natural' unit. As Metternich himself put it, the Empire was composed of 'different provinces united under one sovereignty by reason of historical fact, legal arrangement, measures of prudence or the force of things'. The one common denominator was the dynasty and a purely dynastic argument for the maintenance of the Empire was surely no longer enough in a Europe still smouldering with the ideas of the French Revolution.

Territorially the Habsburg possessions in 1815 can be roughly grouped as follows: the so-called Hereditary Lands (that is Upper and Lower Austria with their environs), the Lands of the Bohemian Crown (including Moravia and what little was left to the Habsburgs of Silesia), the Lands of the Hungarian Crown (including Croatia and Transylvania), and then Galicia and Lombardy-Venetia. In addition, the Habsburgs exercised considerable influence in Germany, where they enjoyed the presidency of the Confederation, and in the Italian Kingdoms of Modena, Parma and Tuscany, which were all ruled by members of the Imperial family. There was thus an enormous administrative problem to be faced from Vienna and this was further complicated by the fact that scattered across these various provinces was a baffling complexity of ethnic groups, whose distribution in no way conformed to the geographical frontiers. The dominant races were the Germans and the Magyars, but there were also Czechs, Slovaks, Croats, Serbs, Slovenes, Italians, Roumanians, Poles, Ruthenes (or Little Russians), Jews and Gypsies, each demanding consideration and all too often protection. Thus the problem of reviving the Empire was not going to be simply one of pleasing the various provinces; it might also involve the formulation of a satisfactory policy towards racial minorities within those provinces. (See map, p. 128.)

Finally, if the would-be administrator turned away from politics for a moment, there was also the problem of economic diversity. How was a progressive and fair-minded policy to be evolved, which could serve equally the needs of primarily agrarian (and still semi-feudal) Austrian and Hungary on the one hand and such relatively developed areas as Lombardy–Venetia and to a lesser extent Bohemia on the other? How too was the problem of a rapidly rising population to be accommodated? The overall rate of population expansion in the Habsburg Lands between 1800 and 1848 was in the region of forty per cent and despite a considerable rate of industrialisation in some areas, particularly Bohemia and Lower Austria, there was bound to be a pressing problem in the country areas as more and more found themselves either landless or dependent on holdings which were either too small or too unfertile to guarantee even a subsistence return. The fragility of this economic situation was to be all too clearly emphasised in the events leading up to the revolutions of 1848.

Added to these general problems were two major personal difficulties, which Metternich would have to face if he was to make any headway in refashioning the internal structure of the Empire. Technically Metternich's brief was only to conduct foreign affairs, at least until 1821 when the Emperor conferred on him the title of Chancellor, which perhaps implied a more general authority. There were many who resented Metternich's success and hoped at least to counter his influence by putting forward a rival who might command the Emperor's confidence on domestic issues as Metternich did on foreign affairs. There was thus a good deal of hostility to Metternich's spasmodic attempts to intervene decisively in domestic affairs, notably from the upper echelons of the bureaucracy, and this was an obstacle that Metternich was never able to surmount, as was amply demonstrated when his critics found their hoped-for champion in the person of Count Kolowrat in the early 1830s. (See pp. 121–2.)

The Emperor's hostility to change

Bureaucratic obstructionism might not in itself have been enough to stop Metternich, but in combination with a second factor it was decisive. That second factor was the temperament of the Emperor Francis. Francis's admiration for Metternich is beyond doubt, but this is not to say that he was in any way subservient to his minister. Francis had a mind of his own – so much so that some historians have questioned the assumption that Habsburg policies of the period can be explained in terms of the 'system of Metternich' and have argued that in fact the 'system', such as it was, was the creation of the Emperor himself. The tragedy from Metternich's point of view was that Francis' convictions utterly precluded the kind of flexible approach that would be necessary to any refashioning of the relationship between Vienna and the subjects of the Empire.

Francis had emerged from the revolutionary period convinced that the key to the future was caution, that change was an unwarrantable gamble and that tried expedients were the best. Policy for him boiled down to the preservation of the old order, or what was left of it, and slamming the doors on all revolutionary influences. His priorities were neatly demonstrated when he rejected economic advice in favour of an Austro–Italian railway line with the words, 'No, no, I will have nothing to do with it, lest the revolution come into the country'. In his rigid conservatism he was unshakeable, for he had the stubborn strength of one who was too able to want to delegate and yet too limited to be able to create on his own. This, combined with his tremendous sense of duty, which also militated against delegation, meant that the Empire would be allowed to experience no policies which were too adventurous for the Emperor's mind to encompass.

Metternich certainly never managed to break through the Emperor's defences and he seems to have resigned himself to this. Even on foreign affairs he was regularly to be heard emphasising the fact that he had little independence.

I know that the Emperor Nicholas has the idea that I can bend to my will the master whom I serve [he remarked to a Russian general in 1829] but this is a false judgement of the Emperor of Austria. His will is strong, and no one can make him do anything that he does not want to do. He overwhelms me with kindness and gives me his confidence; but he does this because I follow the direction which he lays down for me. If I had the misfortune to leave this prescribed path, Prince Metternich would not be minister of foreign affairs for another twenty-four hours.

In domestic affairs the Emperor was quite as cramping and Metternich's description of the fate of one of his reform memoranda sums up to perfection the stifling potential of his master:

I handed it to the Emperor at the beginning of 1817 and he put it into his drawer.

When the Emperor was convalescing after a serious illness in 1827, he sent for me one day at eight o'clock in the morning. When I had taken my place he apologised for calling me so early and then he said: 'I have a confession to make: I am recovering from an illness which I thought might prove fatal. Whilst I was ill I regretted not having looked at your scheme. As soon as I am up, I shall appoint a commission to study it and I would like you to preside. Give me a list of those whom you would like as colleagues.'

On 31 December 1834 I called on the Emperor to offer my New Year greetings 'Once again you see me a repentant sinner,' he said, interrupting me; 'your scheme has still not come out of my drawer. I give you my word that the year 1835 shall not elapse before the plan is set in motion.' Two months later the Emperor was no more.

Small wonder, one may think, that Francis's reign witnessed no adventurous projects in domestic policy and that the breathing space that was won for the Habsburgs by Metternich's diplomacy was not turned to any positive and lasting advantage. But this is not to say that Metternich would necessarily have done much better had he been given a free hand. It is necessary to look critically at his ideas before one can decide whether or not Francis was depriving the Habsburgs of a major opportunity in obstructing the proposals which were set before him.

[17] METTERNICH'S DOMESTIC POLICIES

If Metternich's overall strategy falls easily into two parts, the diplomacy being intended as a prelude to constructive internal reform, so too did his approach to the domestic problem. Here again his plan fell clearly into two phases. First of all he was determined to suppress ideas that he believed to be prejudicial to order and to the general stability of the Empire. This essentially negative policy was then to pave the way for construction. Metternich planned to outmanoeuvre the critics of the Empire by giving it a new dynamism, a new and persuasive justification. He sought to convince the peoples living under Habsburg rule that the advantages of that rule far outweighed its deficiencies.

To this end he urged a policy of greater efficiency in Vienna and the promotion of provincial autonomy so far as was compatible with the essential requirements of the central government. He sought to strike the infinitely delicate balance between over-all efficiency and local self-respect.

Repression

The ideas that Metternich was determined to suppress within the Empire were no different from those which he had set his face against in Europe. It was only logical that he who had called for solidarity between governments in contesting the revolutionary menace should set a vigorous example in the territories for which he was immediately responsible. His suspicions focused firmly on the middle classes, whose 'presumption', he believed, led them to seek for themselves a dominance in society for which they were not 'naturally' suited. From this presumption there flowed a stream of fallacious doctrines, which were bound to prove abortive because they were in defiance of the 'natural order', but which would unleash innumerable problems nonetheless. Most particularly obnoxious to Metternich's mind were the ideas of liberalism and nationalism, the former because it would lead eventually to anarchy as the presumption of the middle classes begat further presumption still further down the social scale and the latter since the majority of areas singled out by the nationalists were by 'nature' unsuited to self government (see Part V). Accordingly Metternich was prepared to use the full range of force tactics to suppress such ideas and minimise their destructive impact, even though his tactics were to impose on Austria a certain notoriety as being the home of censorship, secret police and prison cells.

In fact, historians have not been entirely fair to Metternich, for although he has generally been singled out as the ultimate personification of this repressive system he was not in fact its initiator. Not only had Francis made the Police a separate ministry and encouraged the hysterical 'Jacobin trials' of 1794–5 before Metternich had come into his service, but even before this the Emperor Joseph II had, in the 1780s, instituted a notoriously rigorous secret police service under Pergen. It is also possible that Francis was a good deal more relentless than Metternich over the length of prison sentences for those convicted of political offences, for Stratford Canning, the British diplomatist, wrote after a meeting with an Italian political prisoner, Count Confalonieri, 'I have it on good authority that the Emperor kept the state-prisoners in the fortress of the Spielberg under his own personal control'. And Silvio Pellico, another prisoner in the Spielberg, sent Metternich a copy of his book *Il Mie Prigione* inside the cover of which was written in his own hand, 'to his Highness the prince de Metternich, Imperial Chancellor, in homage with the grateful respect of the author'.

Nonetheless it is clearly true that Metternich believed in repression, albeit as a necessary evil, and that the police under the direction of himself and the Chief of Police, Count Sedlnitzky, were vigorous and thorough. Such state prisons as the Spielberg, Kufstein and Munkács, seemed to many the natural façade of the regime and the dramatic reaction of the Austro–American writer, Charles Sealsfield, to the proliferation of the police was by no means untypical:

since the year 1811 ten thousand Näderer or secret policemen are at work. They are recruited from the lower classes of the merchants, of domestic servants, of workers, nay even of prostitutes, and they form a coalition which traverses the entire Viennese society as the red silk thread runs through the rope of the English navy. You can scarcely pronounce a word at Vienna which would escape them. You have no defense against them and if you take with you your own servants, they become within fourteen days, even against their own will, your traitors.

If the machinery for dealing with actual transgressors was tough, so too were the preventive measures that were taken. Censorship was widespread and obtruded into areas that were not primarily political, as the protests of such literary figures as the Austrian writer Grillparzer make clear. 'Despotism has ruined my literary life', he lamented; and one can sympathise with the lot of a dramatist working in a country where Schiller's

William Tell, admittedly a play dealing with patriotism in a war of liberation, could only be played heavily cut to suit the censor and Shakespeare's *Hamlet* could not be played at all.

Equally under suspicion, along with artists in general, were university teachers. One of the most dreary and depressing aspects of the Metternich period was the hostility felt for thinkers and ideas. The old tag, *cogitat, ergo Jacobinus est*, is sad comment on the defensive timidity of the regime. In Austria itself the government did all it could to ensure the reliability of the universities. Sealsfield painted a soul-destroying picture of academic life in Austria:

free spiritual creation or investigation is completely unrealistic, nay, it is strictly forbidden to the professors. During his studies the student is severely watched over and his professors are official spies. The teacher of religion must hold a confession with the students six times a year. The inclinations, the good and bad qualities, every emotion of the young men, are observed and noted in catalogues from which a copy is sent to the Court Commission for Studies in Vienna, a second to the governor's office and a third remains in the school archive.

Meanwhile Metternich was unhappy about the mood of the universities elsewhere, notably in Germany, as this letter of 1820 shows:

the teaching posts were converted into platforms for radicals, lecturers not only dared to teach openly the most subversive maxims of any religion or social order, but set up assassination as a civic virtue and as a moral principle.

It was in fact in Germany that Metternich pulled off his most dramatically repressive stroke of all, the Carlsbad Decrees, which he successfully piloted through the German Diet in September 1819. This document, passed at least with the appearance of unanimity, committed the member states of the Confederation to total renunciation of the ideas that Metternich had singled out for destruction. Metternich had for some time been supremely uneasy about the climate of opinion in the German states, where certain elements had taken up the causes of liberal and national development in defiance of the conservative nature of the Vienna solution to the German problem. Things had reached a peak in March 1819 when a young, and normally placid, student, Karl Ludwig Sand, had planned and carried out the murder of a German playwright, Kotzebue. The motive was political, for Kotzebue was known to combine with his activities as a dramatist the functions of a Russian spy, and to the radical student groups the rapid conversion of the Tsar Alexander from liberalism to conservatism was a major disappointment. The murder was a fanatical gesture against reaction and repression.

Metternich saw his chance and took it. As he wrote to Gentz, 'there is no time to lose, for the governments are now so terrified that they are willing to act. Soon their fears will be overcome by their weakness'. Accordingly Metternich moved fast. First he conferred in secret with the King of Prussia at Teplitz in July; then with the representatives of the nine major states of the German Confederation at Carlsbad in August; and finally representatives of all the members of the Confederation met at Vienna in September. Throughout the deliberations Metternich played on the fears of the various rulers and if, as many German historians have argued, the final unanimity of the Diet was in part due to bullying and duplicity on Metternich's part there can be little doubt nonetheless that the Kotzebue murder merely clinched for the majority a sense of uneasiness that they had felt for some time.

The Decrees, as they ultimately emerged, can be outlined under four headings. They called for closer supervision of the universities: professors ejected for subversive teaching in any one state were not to be employed in any other and student societies were to be restricted. A general edict provided for preliminary censorship of all books and pamphlets of less than twenty pages and the possibility of further censorship was left to the discretion of the various states themselves. A Central Commission was set up to hunt out demagogues and subverters. And finally, Article 13 of the original Articles of Confederation was 'reinterpreted'. This article, which had allowed for certain constitutional developments within the states, had been seized upon by radicals as a loophole for popular sovereignty. The article was now declared to refer *only* to the representation of Provincial Diets in some form of central State Reichsrat and *not* to any form of popular representation.

This then was the general flavour of Metternich's repression. Subversive ideas and actions were to be stifled by whatever means lay closest to hand so that, out of the void, there might develop a compelling alternative, the newly invigorated Habsburg Empire of Metternich's dream.

The Dream: Efficiency and conciliation

It has already been pointed out that Metternich would find it enormously difficult to alter the traditional structures of government, because of the obsessive caution of the Emperor Francis. That Metternich was aware of the immensity of this obstacle is painfully obvious from the phrasing of the introduction to a memorandum of 1817 in which he advocated a measure of administrative reorganisation.

In my report [he wrote] there is nothing glaring, nothing revolutionary, not a single dangerous principle. No time is less suited than the present for the propagation in any state of reforms in a wide sense of the word. But, happily, the machinery of state is constructed on such good principles that, in a wide sense, there is really nothing in the machinery itself to be altered. Everything that I have proposed concerns first principles as a whole. And here I do not venture on one reform tending to the overthrow of normal forms, but merely a regulation of the parts, and those, indeed, the already existing organic parts of the central authority of the state.

Metternich did make a number of attempts to modify and improve the system, but at no time was he really successful, for the Emperor's lack of enthusiasm made his schemes easy meat for the opposition of the traditionalist bureaucrats, who had little time for change and probably even less for Metternich, whose influence with the Emperor they resented.

Central to Metternich's thinking was his admiration for the Napoleonic administrative system. He felt that the Austrian system lacked a clear division of responsibilities and that as a result the Emperor tended to get bogged down in trivia, which should have been handled and despatched at an infinitely lower level. With this in mind he submitted a memorandum in 1811 in which he suggested the formation of an Imperial Council along the lines of Napoleon's Council of State. Purely advisory, this body would meet at the Emperor's behest to discuss broad issues with a bearing on policy, whilst the traditional Conference of Ministers would concentrate exclusively on executive matters. 'The Council, according to its proper notion, cannot be an executive body. It advises the monarch, in whom all powers are united in his function of making and guarding the laws.' The Emperor was to nominate the members of the Council and to apportion business between it and the Ministerial Conference.

This scheme, although given a token run in 1814, never worked well because of bureaucratic hostility and imperial apathy, but Metternich's attachment to it as a means to greater efficiency was such that he tried it again after Francis's death (p. 123) and was still justifying it to such as would listen after his fall. The following is taken from a letter of 1851:

I have always had in mind as a significant element in the structure of government the existence of a consultative authority which is not saddled with executive power ... the authority must be morally independent, well organised and composed of really able men, if it is to be constructive. If these conditions are met, it will reassure the ministers and give confidence to the people.

A similarly frustrating fate was in store for another of his projects, this time a bid for administrative uniformity, which was given an equally abortive token run in 1817. Metternich proposed that the provinces of the Empire should at last be governed in a systematic way. They should be divided into ethnic groups as far as possible and allocated to the care of one of six central Chancelleries. Such Chancelleries already existed for Hungary and for Transylvania and these were to be joined by four more, one for Bohemia–Moravia–Silesia, one for Austria–Illyria, one for Lombardy–Venetia and one for Galicia.

Coordinating the whole organisation was to be a High Chancellor, who would thus incidentally, if the scheme worked well, be very much the counterbalance to Metternich's influence over foreign affairs that his critics were so eager to create. Yet even this implication was not sufficient to buy bureaucratic support for the plan, which was thus damned from the start. As for the Emperor, he simply would not be persuaded to take a galvanic interest in such schemes; even Metternich's pointed observations to the effect that, unless the administration could be modified to work reasonably effectively with only a minimum of royal application, there was going to be trouble in the not unlikely event of an inadequate succession (Francis's son, Ferdinand, was quite unsuited to rule), failed to jolt the Emperor into a positive interest in even moderate change.

Metternich's attempts to give to the Imperial government a compelling reputation for right-minded efficiency were thus a failure. So too were his attempts to develop a new understanding between the crown and the various provinces under its rule. Again the Emperor Francis is open to criticism, though whether Metternich's plans really contained the seeds of a solution is open to doubt.

There were clearly two ways of approaching the problem of Vienna's relationship with the provinces. Either one might attempt a monumental centralisation of authority, a fusion of all the conflicting elements in the Empire along the lines that had been projected by Joseph II, or one might accept that such a plan was impracticable and seek to establish a more relaxed but nonetheless meaningful relationship between the centre and the provinces by gentler means. This was what Metternich was hoping to do, for he rejected the idea of fusion outright.

How difficult a system of fusion must be in a kingdom which contains so many different languages and races of people, whose provinces were mostly brought together by conquest, follows from the nature of things. The miscarriage of the attempt, and especially its entire repeal by the Emperor Joseph, renders the case still more difficult, so that I am quite convinced that a forcible system of fusion is an empty and dangerous hypothesis.

Metternich's plan, such as it was, is not easy to piece together, particularly since one crucial memorandum (the one to which the Emperor referred in 1827 and 1834: pp. 108–9) has been lost. However, it really divides in two again. Above all else he sought to give the provinces real cause for satisfaction so that the Habsburg dynasty might capitalise on provincial contentment. He hoped to achieve this in part by encouraging the pride of the provinces in themselves and in their own institutions and traditions and in part by giving them a real sense of involvement in the affairs of the Empire as a whole.

The first part of the plan, the stimulation of local contentment, he hoped to achieve by giving as much authority as possible to the Provincial Estates. These were the local aristocracy, who met from time to time in their respective Diets to discuss matters of administrative importance. These Diets, normally comprising two or three chambers to accommodate prelates, magnates and lesser nobility, had become the logical counterpart to the power of Vienna, where the various Chancelleries of the central government transmitted their intentions to the Provinces via the local Governors and their *gubernia*, provincial secretariats made up of professional civil servants.

The tendency of the centralist bureaucrats was generally to whittle away local privileges and in some areas the Estates had actually lapsed but Metternich pressed that they should be revived, arguing that it was doubly dangerous to have some areas enjoying such privileges (notably Hungary) and others not. (According to this policy Provincial Estates were actually revived after the Vienna peace settlement in Tyrol–Vorarlberg, Carniola and Salzburg.) Obviously the Estates must not be allowed to obstruct the prime requirements of the central government, but through being trusted with purely local responsibilities they would develop a self-esteem which would do the Habsburg government no harm and might well redound to its advantage. If each individual province could be brought to feel a debt of gratitude to the open-handedness of the Vienna government, if Vienna could commend itself as the natural centre towards which all eyes turned (and Metternich's desire that this should be so is further evidenced by his consistent patronage of foreign artists, scientists and historians in his desire to make of Vienna a rival to Paris) and if the Habsburgs could acquire a benevolent father-image, much would have been achieved.

The second part of the plan, the attempt to confer on the provinces a greater sense of involvement with the centre, got even less far than the other plans already discussed. At least they all had a token run: no attempt at all was made to put this into practice. Metternich's scheme was outlined in the lost memorandum of 1817 and his line of thought was hinted at in the companion memorandum of that year on provincial administration, for in that he mentioned but did not follow up the idea of 'a central representation of the nation'. Extracts from Metternich's writings after his fall from power give a clearer picture of what he had in mind.

I propose, therefore, a revision of the Diets in order to form a Reichsrat, which would extend from the centre outwards – from the Emperor to the landed proprietors selected – to be completed by the delegates from the different Diets. To this new central point the scrutiny of the budget and of every law which concerns the community will be submitted.

The exact nature of the power of such a body is not made clear, but it is obvious enough from the general tone of Metternich's writings that it would not have enjoyed anything like a veto. It would, however, have served to give the provinces that sense of significance in the affairs of the central government which Metternich had in mind. It would be a further gesture of cooperative intent on the part of the government in Vienna.

And yet it is perhaps too simple to portray Metternich as the frustrated healer of the Habsburg Empire, for it is very doubtful whether his schemes would really have met the case, even had they been given a fair chance. The powers that he would have been prepared to allow the central Reichsrat were scanty indeed and the policy of fostering the provincial estates, whilst relatively safe from Metternich's point of view because they were the preserve of the traditional ruling class, was not really a radical break with tradition and was certainly no solution to the in-

creasingly menacing problem of racial minorities within the
various provinces. It seems not unreasonable to suggest that the
policy that Metternich was advocating without much success
was not so much a constructive departure as a return to the well-
tried negative tactic of 'divide and rule'. In other words, he was
trying to keep the individual provinces loyal to the Habsburgs,
but he was not providing the Empire with any powerfully new
and transcending reasons for its continued existence as a political
unit.

The final irony is that despite their differences over the value
of change as a tactic, there is a marked similarity of view between
Metternich and the Emperor on the ultimate strategy to be employed in keeping the Empire intact. That strategy was to
emphasise the differences between the provinces rather than to
soothe them over. In the words of Francis to the French Ambassador,

my peoples are strange to one another and that is as it should be
They do not get the same sickness at the same time. In France if the
fever comes you are caught by it at the same time. I send the Hungarians into Italy, the Italians into Hungary. They do not understand
one another; indeed they hate one another . . . from their antipathy
will be born order and from their mutual hatred general peace.

In the words of Metternich to a Bourbon émigré,

revolutions would not in our case mean a forest fire. If the Hungarian
revolts . . . we should immediately send the Bohemian against him,
for they hate one another; and after him the Pole, or the German, or
the Italian.

The imagery of the two extracts is different, but the message is
the same, that the concessions Metternich was prepared to offer
were little more than a confidence trick and that the only significant difference between himself and the Emperor was that he
was inclined to package his determination that the Empire
should survive in attractive wrapping paper, whilst Francis saw
no need to disguise his true priorities.

[18] THE CHANGE OF EMPERORS

So far we have looked only at Metternich's attempts to steer his moderate reform policies past the Emperor Francis and his failure to overcome his master's obsessive caution. In March 1835 the Emperor died, however, and it looked to many of Metternich's contemporaries, friend and foe alike, that his real chance had come at last, for Francis's eldest son, Ferdinand, could not be expected to be much more than a cypher. The child of a marriage between first cousins, he was prone to fits of epilepsy and was mentally very retarded, so much so that the unfortunate man has become something of an object lesson to those who delight in the different nuances that historians can give to the same piece of basic evidence. Described by A. J. P. Taylor as 'an imbecile', Ferdinand becomes for the gentler Algernon Cecil 'no worse than a good-natured child', but in either event he was clearly unfitted to rule in the sense that Francis had ruled. There had, in fact, been talk of passing him over in favour of his younger brother, Franz Karl, father of Ferdinand's eventual successor, Franz Joseph, but Metternich had opposed this, partly perhaps because he did not want to brush aside the 'legitimate' successor, partly too perhaps because he saw for himself a chance to dominate in the new situation. Certainly he looked well placed to do so when the text of the Emperor Francis's Last Will and Testament was published.

Emperor Francis's will

This document, although not actually dictated by Metternich, does seem to have been based on a draft prepared by him in 1832. Certainly the combination of conservative caution and the commendations of Metternich that it incorporated seemed to put the new Emperor very much under his control. . . .

Change nothing in the foundations of the structure of the state; govern and change nothing. Apply with an immovable resolution the principles the observance of which has enabled me to guide the monarchy across the storms of a difficult period. [Nothing demon-strates more concisely than this the degree to which Metternich and Francis were at odds with the mood of revolutionary thought. The emphasis is on the 'monarchy' and not the 'people'.]

And then,

bestow on Prince Metternich, my most faithful servant and friend, the trust which I have reposed in him during so many years. Take no decision on public affairs, or respecting persons, without hearing him. I enjoin him, for his part, to show you the same sincerity and faithful devotion as he has always displayed towards me.

If Metternich really had a creative urge, one which had been frustrated by the conservatism of the Emperor Francis, then now was his chance to take command and yet he failed to do so. Why?

The most obvious explanation is that the obstructionism of Francis was replaced by an alternative obstructionism, this time that of a group, which Metternich lacked the power to destroy. The Emperor Francis had indeed envisaged a future in which Metternich would play a dominant role, but he had at the same time groomed his youngest brother, Ludwig (often known as Louis), to assist the Emperor Ferdinand too. The trouble was that Ludwig was generally believed to be the least talented of Francis's brothers and the rumour (possibly true) easily circu-lated that Metternich had pressed for his selection simply because he would find him easy to dominate. Thus it was that a jealous trio of ambitious and penetrating critics was on hand to make sure that Metternich went no further than was absolutely necessary as he set about adapting the government machine to the demands of the new situation.

Opposition to Metternich

Metternich's powerful critics were the Archdukes Charles and John (brothers of Francis) and the Bohemian bureaucrat, Count Anton Kolowrat. The opposition of the Archdukes to Metternich went back a long way. They resented his influence at Vienna, particularly so since both had been driven from the capital by Francis, with whom they had had differences of opinion. Unfortunately for Metternich both were strong characters, vital and able in their different ways, Charles a forceful soldier and John an eloquent liberal. The enmity of Kolowrat was of more recent growth. He had risen to influence during the late twenties and had made a name for himself as Finance Minister, his most dramatic achievement in this field having been the prediction of a budget surplus for 1831, though the untimely expenses incurred in the countering of the 1830 revolutions had denied him the ultimate gratification of seeing his prediction come true. A man of moody temper, he was a prickly customer, and he disagreed with Metternich on a number of issues.

In particular he was opposed to the broad concept of Metternich's diplomacy on the grounds that the Austrian economy simply could not stand the cost of the military establishment that Metternich demanded as a security against the revolution *wherever it might show itself*. (Compare Metternich's letter to the Emperor, October 1829, pp. 91–2.) Furthermore, he was a bureaucrat of the Josephinian school and had little liking for Metternich's tendency towards decentralisation in internal administration. Then again, also in the tradition of Joseph, he was opposed to the steadily increasing ultramontane emphasis of Metternich's religious thinking. But most significant of all probably, he was himself ambitious and came to see himself as the rightful director of domestic affairs, the logical counterpart to Metternich and his dominant influence in foreign affairs, and he was encouraged in this belief by the countless voices which sought if not the removal of Metternich, then at least the elevation of an effective rival. If Kolowrat seems to lack consistency at times (and certainly his avowed liberalism does not stand up to analysis) it is surely because he followed no principled programme, but tended rather to extemporise from day to day to find a line that would balk his arch-opponent. As Kübeck put it, Kolowrat became 'the plaything of certain highly-placed intriguers, who egg him on'.

Francis had mentioned none of these men in his last will and testament, however, and it was up to Metternich and Ludwig to make the first move. Metternich in fact reverted to the ideas which he had failed to implement effectively under Francis. He suggested a distinction between the executive and consultative aspects of government, as he had done in 1811. There was to be a State Conference, chaired by himself and in command of the executive, and there was to be a State Council whose function was to be mainly advisory. Then, referring back to 1817, there was perhaps to be a Reichsrat too.

It was not to be, however; the Archdukes Charles and John, together with the affronted Kolowrat, who looked likely to lose all pretence of parity with Metternich if not all hope of any post in Vienna whatsoever, prevailed upon Ludwig to apply the brake. Metternich, they argued, was aiming to become a dictator, to usurp the prerogatives of the imperial family. Once more Metternich's plans crumbled. The Reichsrat was scrapped, the State Council remained but was of little use without an effective executive, and all hope of the latter was destroyed when Ludwig was made president (in lieu of Ferdinand) of the State Conference, the other members of which were to be Franz Karl (as heir apparent and father of the likely heir to the throne in the next generation), Metternich and Kolowrat. Once again the Austrian executive was condemned to immobility. As president Ludwig had little to say and was quite incapable of giving a lead, Franz Karl was ineffectual and the floor was thus left to Metternich and Kolowrat, who more or less cancelled one another out. The chances of agreement and movement were negligible. As Dr Macartney aptly puts it, 'the only two members of the Conference who performed their duties quite adequately were Ferdinand himself, and Franz Karl; they had nothing to do, and that is what they did'.

Once again then Metternich's schemes for reform had yielded to powerful resistance and yet the combination that defeated him in 1836 was not so powerful as the lone resistance of Francis. The men who outmanoeuvred Metternich in 1836 were not the legitimate authority. To a very considerable extent Metternich himself had that advantage. One may well wonder then why it was that Metternich put up so little fight on behalf of his plans. He himself was fond of pointing out that he had no desire to be a Richelieu and that Austria was not the place for 'mayors of the palace', but it is hard to resist the conclusion that had he been really convinced that his solutions were the right ones, he might have risked a tougher line in the crucial months following Francis's death. Or was it simply that his fear of revolution was such that he dared not risk exposing to general view a rift in the highest levels of the administration; that he succumbed to his opponents in order to maintain at least the appearance of solidarity?

[19] THE VOR MÄRZ

Historians have seldom, if ever, coined a more depressing phrase with which to describe a period than the '*Vor März*' or 'Pre-March'. Everything that happened in the period ranging from the death of Francis in February 1835 to the outbreak of the Vienna revolution in March 1848 is thus seen as significant only in so far as it is part of a period of suspended animation, part of the build-up to the inevitable explosion. And yet the phrase accords well enough with Metternich's own thinking, for he had hinted to Francis on several occasions that the Habsburg dynasty would find it hard to survive under the inadequate Ferdinand unless some cautious but purposeful reform of the system of government were undertaken. Such reform had been inhibited by Francis and blocked by the machinations of Kolowrat and the Archdukes John and Charles. Now the dynasty was to pay the price that Metternich had predicted it would pay.

Administration

Metternich really gave up hope after the defeat of his plans in 1836. Looking back on the years 1835–48, he picked on a number of factors as contributory to failure. Above all he regretted the failure to instill some speed and energy into government. 'One of the great obstacles with which I have had to battle during my ministry has been the lack of energy in the internal administration.' It was for this reason that Metternich was so eager for a clearer apportionment of duties between the advisory consultative branch of government and the executive branch. On the subject of the executive, remarkably guarded though the Memoirs arc on the subject of Kolowrat, he did find his rival wanting. Kolowrat, concluded Metternich, was 'fundamentally honest, but having come up through the bureaucracy he could not transcend it'. 'Count Kolowrat was born to be an instrument and not a director.' Here in a nutshell was Metternich's prime grievance, that the traditionally minded bureaucrat type was geared to ponderous and cumbersome procedures and was inflexibly hostile to change. These factors, probably consolidated by a sulky resentment of Metternich as a 'foreigner', spelt doom to Metternich's programme. The result was the administrative stagnation of the Vor März.

The Economy

And yet it would be a mistake to assume that no progress of any kind was made in the Empire during these years. They were in many ways exciting years from an economic point of view. It was during the thirties and forties that Austria began to develop a railway system: she had over one thousand kilometres of track by 1848. Industry in the Empire, or more particularly in Austria, Bohemia and Lombardy–Venetia, became rapidly more mechanised. Traditional products like textiles, coal and iron, increased their output and new processes were being introduced as well, notably sugar refining.

But all this was not achieved without the growth of further symptoms of discontent. Urban conditions were poor: working hours were long (often thirteen to sixteen hours per day for adults and twelve and a half for children), accommodation was lacking (most startling was the development of the *Bettgeher*, an institution which enabled the individual to hire a bed by the hour!), and unemployment was a commonplace, partly because a general reluctance to invest in industry meant that most projects were perilously short of capital security and partly because the development of machines left many redundant. (There was a series of epidemics of machine smashing during the mid-forties.) Meanwhile peasant grievances were mounting too, most notably amongst those whose holdings were too small to give adequate security to their families but also amongst richer peasants who bitterly resented the survival of the 'robot', the traditional labour service owed by tenant to master, and also the lack of security of tenure in some instances.

Metternich, professional pessimist though he may have become by the 1840s, was increasingly of the opinion that Austria had somehow missed the boat economically. He was particularly critical of the State Conference's refusal of an invitation to join the German Zollverein in 1841 (p. 160), for he was painfully aware of the fact that Prussia was drawing away from Austria in terms of economic strength. Again the essence of his reproach was the passivity of Government policy:

while in the centre of the industrial movement in Germany [he wrote in 1840] I observed the forces in operation, the direction which they were taking; I felt clearly that we were in a position of inferiority because we had no commercial policy of our own, no policy which was definitely Austrian, and in harmony with the situation. I felt that our policy was passive in contrast to the incessant activity which I noticed elsewhere.

He might also have added that only a more dynamic economic policy could solve the pressing problem of government finance, for the yield of taxation was quite inadequate for the needs of government and the Vor März régime really made do on an unhealthy diet of borrowing, unpopular indirect taxes, underspending on the army and underpaying the civil service.

The development of articulate opposition

Small wonder then that the atmosphere of the 1840s was one of mounting criticism. What was perhaps more important, however, was the nature of that criticism. It was not just the depressed elements in society which were vocal: nor was it just the students: there were a number of organised groups developing whose membership was influential and distinguished. Most impressive, because of the heterogeneous nature of its membership, was the Juridischer–Politischer Leseverein (the Juridical–Political reading circle), which was founded in 1842. In this organisation were to be found aristocrats, professors, lawyers, businessmen, a wide range of people amongst whom were many who were to become ministers in the years following 1848 – Thun, Bach and Schmerling, to name but a few. Their discussions were regularly devoted to ideas for constitutional reform.

Government response to such activities was feeble. Indeed Kolowrat actually protected the Leseverein, probably mainly to spite Metternich who disapproved of it, and Metternich's wife Melanie has left us a picture of Metternich in 1840 in which he appears virtually to have opted out of internal affairs altogether.

He is very busy with foreign affairs; he leaves internal questions alone as much as he possibly can for the moment and he seems to me not to wish to deal with things where he finds only disagreeables and opposition which wears him out. He has no strength to fight as he had done in the past.

The truth of the matter was that the government was increasingly at a loss, increasingly aware of its own inadequacy. There was no such unanimous faith in the validity of what was being done as had sustained Francis and Metternich in the previous decades. All was uncertainty, an illogical interplay of concession and repression, as the government became daily more confused. There was even a strong revival of ultramontane thinking in court circles – the Jesuits were readmitted to the Empire and the young Franz Joseph was tutored by, among others, von Rauscher, the main evangelist of the 'pious' trend – was this, too, symptomatic of the generally dwindling faith in human solutions? In the last resort the government lacked the confidence in itself to put up much of a fight when the challenge came in March 1848. In this sense the gloomy pessimism of the label, Vor März, is amply justified.

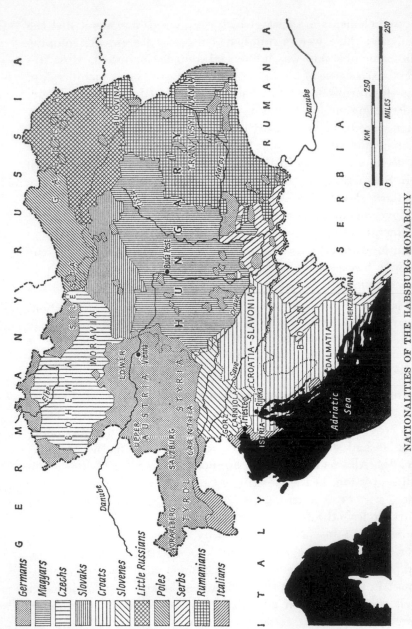

NATIONALITIES OF THE HABSBURG MONARCHY

(reproduced from *The Habsburg Monarchy* by A. J. P. Taylor, published by Hamish Hamilton)

Germans
Magyars
Czechs
Slovaks
Croats
Slovenes
Little Russians
Poles
Serbs
Rumanians
Italians

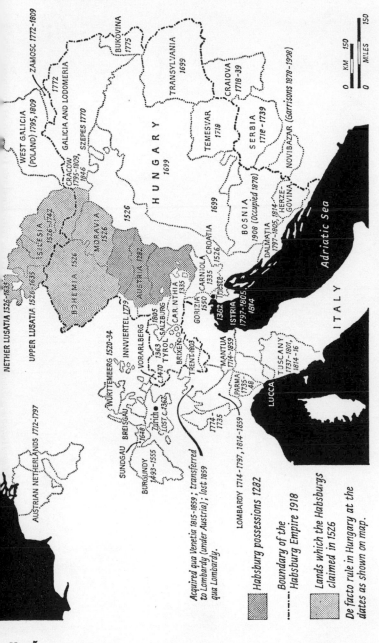

THE GROWTH OF THE HABSBURG EMPIRE

(reproduced from *The Habsburg Empire* by C. A. Macartney, published by Weidenfeld and Nicolson)

PART V
The Forces of Change

[20] COLLAPSE OF SOLIDARITY

The year 1848 stamped the word 'failure' on Metternich's tactics, both in the field of diplomacy and in that of provincial administration. Just as the failure of Russia to intervene promptly against the revolutions in Europe marked the collapse of the solidarity of the trio of powers east of the Rhine, which Metternich had so dramatically recovered by the treaty of München-grätz in 1833 and upon which his diplomacy had come to depend, so did the sequence of revolt in Austria itself and in Germany, Italy, Hungary, Bohemia and Galicia, mark the failure of his attempt to provide a new justification for Habsburg rule in these areas and it is at his attempts to restore Habsburg prestige in the provinces of the Empire and the reasons for his failure that this chapter will look.

Essentially his domestic policies were conceived in terms of a balance. On the one hand he was committed to the repression of dangerous and subversive ideas and to the belief that government to be good must be strong. To this end he was prepared to use the widest variety of techniques, ranging from his ideal of rational persuasion through to the relentless alternatives of police action and in areas of conflicting national interests the unattractive tactic of stimulating racial animosities in order to prevent any unanimous challenge to Habsburg authority. On the other hand, however, he hoped to justify his unyielding defence of legitimate authority by providing the subjects of the Emperor with real benefits, not only the obvious advantages of order and

stability but also perhaps material benefits such as would come
with economic growth and improved facilities for trade. The
great tragedy was that such constructive elements as were to be
found in his policies in practice were generally either too scanty
or too late or both. Thus the picture that predominated and
which clamped itself on the contemporary mind was one of
negative reaction, one where such creativity as there was was
simply overshadowed by the lowering and omnipresent signs of
repression.

It must be remembered too, when looking at the relationship
of the Vienna government with the provinces, that Metternich
had no monopoly of power in this and that often the decisions
that were taken were either none of his doing or actually in defiance of his considered opinions. Thus it is very much more
difficult to measure Metternich's success or failure in the domestic
affairs of the Empire than it is to assess his diplomatic significance. In the reviews of events in Bohemia, in Hungary, in
Galicia, in Italy and in Germany, that follow, Metternich is not
always the central figure that he was in diplomacy therefore.

[21] BOHEMIA

Bohemia is probably the province on which Metternich had the
least impact. By comparison with Hungary, Galicia, Italy, and
Germany, the Bohemian lands were relatively easy to control
and as a result Metternich was not personally involved with
their administration to any great extent. Furthermore, his great
rival, Kolowrat, was himself a Czech and tended understandably
to command attention on the subject of his native land. There
were, however, divisive forces developing in Bohemia, if little
actual separatism, and these were to lead to a clash of arms in
Prague in June 1848.

Bohemian docility towards Habsburg rule was a well established tradition. The real fire had been knocked out of the

Bohemians at the start of the seventeenth century and there had
been no major challenge since then. The Habsburgs had in fact
acquired the Bohemian crown in 1526, on the death of the last
of the Jagiellon kings, Louis, in battle with the Turks – this was
one of the Habsburgs, many successful conquests by marriage,
for Louis left only a sister to succeed him and she was already
married to Ferdinand, the younger brother of the Habsburg
Emperor, Charles V. The disciplining of Bohemia came some
years later, during the Thirty Years' War, and in 1627 Ferdinand
II revised the Bohemian constitution and put the Bohemian
Diet in the place where it belonged as far as he was concerned.
From then on it was little more than a mechanism for approving,
apportioning and collecting the taxes demanded by the king. At
the same time the succession was declared hereditary in both the
male *and* female lines of the Habsburg dynasty. The domesti-
cation of the Bohemian lands was then really completed by
Maria Theresa and Joseph II who virtually made a single administrative unit out of the lands of Austria and Bohemia combined.
A minor challenge was thrown out by the Bohemian Diet in
1791, when the death and failure of Joseph II seemed to invite
such a gesture (voices were heard demanding a return to the
constitutional situation that had existed prior to 1627), but
Leopold was not to be intimidated and he declared the year 1764
the one to which he was prepared to revert. Since most of Maria
Theresa's administrative reforms had gone through by that year
this was not a significant concession and the Diet relapsed into
passivity once more. During the Napoleonic wars Austria got
substantial assistance from Bohemia, and that without much
difficulty.

Once the wars were over, however, two contentious issues
came increasingly to the fore in Bohemia, one a long standing
problem, the other not altogether new but suddenly gaining
unprecedented impetus.

Economic unrest

The first of these problems was an economic one. Superficially
Bohemia was impressive from an economic point of view in that
she had taken the lead in industrialisation during the late eighteenth century. Her main product was textiles and the 1830s
saw a further dramatic development of the textile industry with
a rapid conversion to steam-driven labour saving machinery. By
1841 there were 219 steam-driven machines operating in the
whole Monarchy, of which 156 were in Bohemia and Moravia–
Silesia. The other major textile producing area was Lower
Austria and the degree to which the two areas were increasing
their interest in the industry is clearly reflected in the fact that
between 1835 and 1842 imports of cotton yarn into the Monarchy
increased eight-fold and imports of raw cotton trebled. Meanwhile the beginnings of railway development also stimulated iron
industries and Bohemian iron production trebled in the period
1820–48. Against this, however, has to be set the fact that
Bohemia had undergone a very rapid population expansion; the
result of this was that there was considerable unemployment in
her towns (the population of Prague was over 100 000 by 1848)
and the peasant population felt itself increasingly under pressure
with more mouths to feed and holdings often totally inadequate.
Thus there was a constant undercurrent of economic unrest
which tended to become dangerous in times of abnormal strain.

Problem of Czech revival

The other problem was a racial one and the escalation of this
issue was the most startling aspect of the period 1815–48 in the
Bohemian lands. These lands were predominantly Czech, but
there was a substantial number of Germans living there as well,
especially in the urban areas. Furthermore, the tendency since
the Habsburg victory over the Bohemians in 1619 (at the battle
of White Mountain) had been more and more towards German-
ising the Czechs. During the eighteenth century it had become
established, without significant protest, that German should be

BOHEMIA 135

the language of administration and that it should be compulsory in schools. Meanwhile the Czech language itself, or the variety of dialects that comprised it, was being reduced to the status of a peasant lingo.

Almost imperceptibly there began to develop a vital intellectual interest in the Czech tradition in particular and the Slav tradition as a whole, as the pressures of war receded. As early as 1791 the Emperor Leopold had founded a chair of Czech at Prague university and there followed a remarkable burgeoning of Czech/Slav vitality. Dobrovsky (1753–1829) started a researching trend with his History of the Czech Language and his Czech Grammar; these were followed by the History of Czech Literature and the Czech Dictionary of Jungmann (1773–1847), the latter work running to five volumes and 4500 pages in all, and a History of Slav Languages and Literature and a work on Slav Antiquities by Safárik (1795–1891). Out of this analytical school there followed logically enough the vast History of Bohemia by Palacký (1798–1876), which he eventually took only to the year 1526 in the ten volumes that he completed, and the beginnings of a Czech artistic renascence with the epic poem *Daughter of Slava* by Kollar (1793–1852) and the music of Skroup (1801–62), who composed the first Czech opera and also the Czech national anthem 'Where is my home'.

For a long time the Habsburg government smiled on this Czech revival. To the emperor Francis it served the purpose of giving the Czechs a pride in themselves which he might be able to mobilise should the German element in Bohemia cause him any difficulty, to Metternich it looked the harmless sort of playing with local traditionalism that he liked to encourage and to Kolowrat it afforded an ideal opportunity to pose as the enlightened champion of his compatriots' interests. However, the movement went further than mere harmless escapism and by the 1840s it was beginning to threaten the traditional Bohemian stability. As Metternich regretfully put it in 1843, 'Czechism is a tendency which, if things take their ordinary course, only leads to small aberrations, but in an epoch of general excitement it works like bean-salad in a cholera epidemic'.

The new enthusiasm for Czech traditions had a doubly unsettling effect. Within the Bohemian lands it led to racial tension,
for the German minority, previously fairly content with the
support it had been getting from Vienna, now began to feel
acutely ill at ease as the flood of Czech literature began to lead
on to historical claims which hinted strongly at the primacy of
the Czech peoples. 'We were in existence before Austria', claimed
Palacky, 'and we will still be here after she is gone.' As far as the
Empire was concerned there were alarming developments too.
During the forties the Bohemian Diet once again began to show
signs of resistance, pressing in 1842 for tax reforms and then
moving on to review the whole issue of Bohemia's constitutional
rights. Meanwhile a lively Czech journalist, Havliček. began a
steady campaign for a measure of self-government for Bohemia.

By 1848 the situation had become very difficult indeed, for
the futility of the policy of fostering rival national spirits in the
expectation that they would simply neutralise one another had been
made abundantly clear. Both the Bohemian Germans and the Bohemian Czechs still looked loyally to Vienna, but they demanded of
Vienna rival courses of action which were totally incompatible. The
German minority tended to welcome the calling of the Frankfort
Parliament in 1848, believing that their security against the Czech
majority in Bohemia lay in Austria's becoming part of a *grossdeutsch* unit (pp. 156–7), a thing which the dynasty had no desire
to do, whereas the Czechs were totally opposed to Austria's becoming submerged in 'Germany' and argued that her future lay
in her leading a multi-national federal state in eastern Europe as
a bastion against Russian expansion. As Havliček truculently
put it, 'Austria will be what we want her to be, or she will cease
to be'. This Panslav idea, that Austria's future lay in her abandoning her role in Germany and in cultivating the interests of
the Slav races, was equally one that the dynasty had no time
for.

Thus by 1848 the traditional passivity of Bohemia had been
ripped asunder as the rivalry of Czechs and Germans was forced
to the fore and the economic crisis of 1846–7, where a food
shortage was followed by a credit slump and a sequence of

closures in the cotton industry, simply added to the fires of discontent.

The government in Vienna had no solution to offer. In allowing 'Czechism' its head they had, if anything, made the situation worse than it had been in 1791 after the excesses of Joseph II in the opposite direction of Germanisation. There was the negative satisfaction to be had that Bohemia was now so divided that it was relatively easy to crush the Prague rising when it came, but this was surely no credit to the government and the fact remained that the Germans and Czechs had been forced apart to such an extent that each group was now demanding from Vienna something that it was not prepared to give, either Austrian commitment to a grossdeutsch state or to a Panslav federation. How much longer the Habsburgs could continue to dominate an area where they were not prepared to satisfy either of the dominant interests was anybody's guess.

[22] HUNGARY

Whereas Bohemian resistance to Vienna was slow to develop the mood of Hungary gave the Habsburgs ample cause for alarm throughout the period of Metternich. It was not until 1825, however, that Metternich was personally involved with Hungary to any great extent, but what he saw during that year filled him with gloom. 'In Hungary', he wrote, 'I encounter all those things on which during my whole public life, and especially during the last ten years, I have made war.' From then on he was intermittently at war with the forces of discontent in Hungary. His approach was a tough one on the whole. He was not to be pushed into change if he could avoid it, though in the final years of his influence there did develop a much more concessionary policy towards Hungary. The tantalising question, one which defies an answer, is whether or not an earlier move to concession on Metternich's part would have prevented the development of those extremist currents in Hungary which ultimately drove the country to revolution and civil war in 1848-9.

Hungary had presented problems to the Habsburgs from the very start of their rule there. As with Bohemia the Habsburg chance had come in 1526 with the death of Louis Jagiellon, who was king of both Hungary and Bohemia (p. 133). But whereas the various estates of the Bohemian lands had accepted the Habsburg succession, the Hungarian nobility had divided. A few had supported the Habsburg claim, but the majority had elected a 'national' king, John Zapyola. This division, followed by a succession of Turkish conquests in Hungary, had left the Habsburgs in control of only a small portion of the Hungarian lands and it was not until the Habsburgs were able to drive the Turks back in the later part of the seventeenth century that their authority in Hungary began to be consolidated. In 1683 the Hungarian Diet at last confirmed the Habsburg succession in the male line and eventually in 1723 it registered the Pragmatic Sanction of the Emperor Charles VI and thereby recognised the succession in the female line too. Thus at last the Habsburgs were acknowledged rulers of the whole complex of the Hungarian lands, the main administrative divisions of which were Hungary itself, Croatia and Transylvania, each with its own Diet. Scattered across these Hungarian lands were a confusion of races in which the Magyars (a term used loosely to describe both the descendants of the original 'Hungarians' and those of other races who had adopted their [Magyar] language) predominated numerically over Slovaks, Croats, Serbs, Ruthenes, Roumanians, Germans, Jews and Gypsies.

The Diets

The Hungarians managed to maintain a measure of independence for themselves which was strikingly in contrast to the subservience of the Bohemians. Technically the old Hungarian constitution demanded that the Diet should be summoned every three years and that legislation could only be implemented by common consent of the monarch and the Estates. The Habsburgs got round this to a considerable extent during the eighteenth century. They did not call the Diet regularly and they often by-passed its legislative function by ruling by Rescripts (or Procla-mations), but the nobility never lost their determination to re-tain a meaningful role for the Diet and after the death of Joseph II they forced Leopold to reiterate all the traditional rights to which they were entitled. In the years that followed the Diet did indeed meet fairly regularly, for the Habsburgs were dependent on the goodwill of the Hungarians for money and men during the war period, but in 1811 cooperation jolted to a halt. The Hungarians refused to accept the fiscal measures implemented in Austria by Count Wallis to save the crown from bankruptcy (p. 15) and eventually Francis dissolved the Diet and forced the measures through by decree, pending the convocation of the next Diet, which did not in fact meet until 1825. By this time the difficulties involved in getting men and money out of Hungary had convinced both the Emperor and Metternich that they had no alternative but to try for a reconciliation. It was the mood of this Diet that drove Metternich to his gloomy conclusions about the state of Hungary mentioned above.

Although the 1825 Diet, which met intermittently over two years, achieved little that was positive or tangible, it did empha-sise three powerful trends in Hungarian thinking. First, there was an understandable desire to ensure for the Diet a more meaningful role in the direction of Hungarian affairs. Second, there was a considerable sense of economic frustration: Austrian tariff policies were unpopular, favouring as they did Austrian goods at the expense of Hungarian, and there was a strong urge to explore new outlets for Hungarian products, the more so since the high prices commanded by Hungarian wheat under the terms of Napoleon's Continental System had fallen off disastrously with the return of Odessa wheat to the market. Finally, there was developing a rapidly increasing enthusiasm for the Magyar language. There had been a series of abortive attempts made from 1791 onwards to get it accepted as the language of admini-stration in place of Latin and this trend was matched by an up-surge of Magyar literature, notably the nationalist epic, *The*

Flight of Zalan by Vörösmarty, which had much the same impact
on the Magyar national consciousness as had Kollar's *Daughter
of Slava* on the Czech. The demand for the recognition of Magyar
as the administrative language, although unsuccessful again in
1825, was to make real progress in the thirties and forties.

Metternich's reaction to these trends was uniformly hostile.
His inveterate suspicion of opposition parties found no exception
here. Indeed when he came to look back on developments over
the years 1825–37 he drew his standard conclusion: 'as always
happens with liberal organisations, the opposition has revealed
radical and demagogic practices and tendencies'. Never missing
a chance to expound on the shallowness of liberal thinking,
Metternich preferred to champion Hungary's 'historic rights', to
eulogise the old medieval constitution which the Habsburgs had
got round so often before and would doubtless evade again. 'That
which has defied the storms of time for eight centuries has proved
its strength.' A pious respect for tradition was thus to be paraded
as an excuse for rejecting even the more moderate requests of
the progressives.

On the economic issue, Metternich was less intransigent but
very cautious. He was not unwilling to listen to arguments for a
rethinking of the Austrian tariff system, but he was not at all
enthusiastic about some of the local projects that were in the air,
notably a plan to build a bridge over the Danube to link the
towns of Buda and Pest, for such projects, he rather churlishly
argued, were purely 'national' in character and would therefore
tend to draw the focus of Hungarian attention away from
Vienna.

As for the linguistic issue, he was thoroughly opposed to the
uniform application of the Magyar tongue throughout the Hungarian lands, for if this were achieved it would further the cause
of Hungarian solidarity and blur over the racial differences and
animosities on which the Habsburgs so often counted to keep
their provinces under control.

Conflict with Széchenyi

Metternich's dampening response to the mood of the Diet of
1825–7 brought him into conflict with its most colourful and
influential figure, Count István Széchenyi. This was in many
ways unfortunate, for Széchenyi had much to offer, not only to
Hungary but also to Vienna, and it may well be that Metternich
would have been better advised to patronise the new leader of
the opposition rather than block him, for Széchenyi's failure to
prevail opened the way for more radical and intransigent leaders
of Hungarian opinion in later years, most notably Lajos Kossuth.

Széchenyi was an attractive figure, a lively character of aristo-
cratic birth, a fluent writer and a man passionately dedicated to
the interests of his country. After a career in the Habsburg
armies, in which military dash was well laced with a highly
romantic and confusing love life, he returned to Hungary where
he quickly caught the popular imagination of the Diet through
two dramatic gestures. First of all he spoke there in his native
tongue rather than the traditional Latin and secondly he offered
a year's income from his estates to help float a National Academy
for the cultivation of the Magyar language. From such beginnings
he went on to unleash a stream of progressive schemes for Hungary. He launched the idea of the casinos – intellectual clubs
where liberal ideas might be discussed – which spread like wild-
fire. (Széchenyi purposely avoided the word 'club' because of its
revolutionary overtones with reference to the French Revolution.) He propounded a host of economic schemes, including the
projected bridge to link Buda with Pest and a plan to make the
Danube more navigable. He pleaded for a more meaningful role
for the Diet and, perhaps most important of all, he rejected the
medieval constitution as anachronistic and urged the nobility to
renounce their exemption from taxation in the interests of the
nation as a whole, for he saw all too clearly that the traditional
structure of Hungarian society, with its unusually large and
generally privileged noble class (Hungary and Galicia were remarkable for a high proportion of lesser nobility: in Hungary
there were some 60 000 families of them, often extremely poor)

and its reputation for peasant distress, could only be brought into line with the demands of common sense by a radical re-thinking of policies and priorities. His general ideas he outlined in two important books, *Hitel* (Credit) which appeared in 1830 and *Vilag* (Light) which followed in 1831.

But for all this Széchenyi was never separatist by intent. He was a loyal and devoted servant of the Habsburg monarchy. What he was trying to do was to modernise Hungary within the Habsburg structure and had the government in Vienna been willing or able to meet him on this then the subsequent radicalism of Kossuth might conceivably have been avoided.

Belated conciliation

Be that as it may, the policy of the State Conference after Francis's death was an uncompromising one. In his 1837 memo-randum on Hungary Metternich proclaimed menacingly, 'today Hungary is not being governed; she must be governed and then we shall see some action'. What was needed, he argued, was a spell of 'salutary terror' to 'enlighten' the people and sure enough a series of arrests followed, the most prestigious victims being Kossuth and the Transylvanian reformer Baron Wesselényi. Meanwhile, even before Metternich had stepped up the policy of repression, Kolowrat had already made considerable headway with another standard Habsburg defence policy. In order to counteract the upsurge of Magyar feeling he had espoused the cause of Croat national sentiment and in particular he had patronised a lively if crude literary talent in the person of Ljudevit Gaj. Gaj, who had been strongly influenced by the Panslav thinking of Kollar, envisaged a Kingdom of Illyria in which the southern Slavs (Croats, Serbs, Slovenes and Bulgars) should find unity under Habsburg patronage and in January 1835 he was authorised by Kolowrat to start his own newspaper, the *Croat News*, which then became the *Illyrian News* the following year.

With Kossuth in gaol and Gaj fulminating in the south the chances of constructive cooperation between the Emperor and

his Magyar subjects looked slight, but then there came a somewhat baffling change of policy, for repression and the stimulation
of the Croat movement were abruptly called off in 1841. It is
surely too facile to argue, as does a recent biographer of Széchenyi, that Metternich had become cocksure as a result of his
success in outmanoeuvring Mehemet Ali in 1839–40. A more
likely view is that this incident had reminded him of how dependent he was on Hungarian goodwill for arms and men, whilst
at the same time it had become clear that Gaj's plans were not
having the hoped for effect, for the Serbs in particular were
clearly hostile to Austria and were more inclined to court
Russian protection. The Illyrian idea was thus hastily abandoned
by the authorities in Vienna.

Now at last there commenced something like a concessionary
policy in Hungary, though the defensive mentality was still the
dominant feature in the thinking of Vienna. Metternich's vigilance was still much in evidence as he reviewed the situation in
1844:

although the fire of revolution has not broken out it smoulders on
and if the elements of destruction are not checked they will transform
the old structure into a heap of cinders. The saving operation is under
way; but it must be pursued to a finish, because half measures will
lead inevitably to revolution.

But in the same review he did have some positive suggestions to
make, notably that by a policy of enlightened assistance to the
economy (through government planning of roads, railways,
canals and so on) the Vienna government might outmanoeuvre
the opposition.

If the Emperor presents himself to the next Diet in this way, and if
in the interim the country is governed with a firm hand, the intrigues
of the parties, their hollow theories and their sterile polemics will go
up in smoke before the energetic attitude of the government.

This was an altogether more constructive approach and in the
Diet of 1844 the Vienna government lent its support to a body
of moderate reformers under Count György Apponyi, who proceeded to develop a cautious reform programme which attracted

a steadily increasing number of supporters through to 1848, so much so that it looked as though the wind might be taken out of the radicals' sails.

The story of Kossuth's Magyar revolution of 1848 lies beyond the confines of this book, but his fortunes in the years immediately preceding 1848 are of relevance to any analysis of Metternich's Hungarian policies. As part of his conciliatory tendency during the forties Metternich allowed Kossuth to edit his own newspaper, the *Pesti Hirlap*, after his release from prison in 1841. Kossuth used the paper to popularise his view that what was wrong in Hungary was generally the fault of Vienna, rather than, as Széchenyi had suggested, at least in part the result of the backwardness and selfishness of the Hungarian nobility. By 1848 the government was, through a measure of concession to the idea of reform, beginning to weaken Kossuth's case and he might never have succeeded in raising a revolt against Vienna had it not been for the fortunate incidence of economic crisis in 1847–8 and the catalytic impact of Metternich's personal downfall in March 1848. One can only wonder whether the relative success of the Vienna government's concessionary policies of the mid-forties, involving as they did a determination to improve communications within Hungary, a more influential role for the Diet and the taxation of noble land, might not have destroyed Kossuth's kind altogether had they been implemented at an earlier date.

Metternich himself did not think so, for in October 1848, after his flight to London, he wrote of Széchenyi to Disraeli in terms both smug and imperturbable:

idealist and man of action rolled into one; heated but high-minded patriot; ambitious both for the general good and for himself, it was he who introduced steam power into Hungary; horse racing; clubs called casinos and the idea of Hungarian nationality, fostered by the spreading of the Hungarian language that was spoken only by the peasants until 1825. . . . Count Széchenyi suddenly got to the point where truth which had hitherto eluded him appeared naked before him. He went mad and is at present in a mental home outside Vienna. The doctors have not given up hope of curing him and I share their optimism in view of his current condition. He has moments of lucidity when he looks back into the past. 'Prince Metternich has always told me how wrong I have been. He has warned me not to interfere with the foundations of a building lest it collapse. I have failed to profit from his advice. I have destroyed my own country.' Then he lapses into madness again.

And yet for all this it is arguable that Metternich was closer to success in Hungary in the period 1844–8 when he was considering something not unlike the programme urged on him by Széchenyi in the late twenties than he had been in the period during which he was committed to repression and no compensations. Had the programme of controlled change got under way earlier Kossuth might have found it more difficult to stage a significant challenge to Vienna in 1848.

[23] GALICIA

The Habsburgs' authority in Galicia was of much more recent origin than their rule in Bohemia and Hungary. During the second half of the eighteenth century Russia, Prussia and Austria had negotiated three successive partition treaties by the terms of which they shared between them the territories of the helpless Polish crown. Austria's most permanent gains came from the first partition treaty of 1772 by which she acquired Eastern Galicia, a large triangle based on the Carpathians. (Her position in this area was further consolidated in 1775, when the Bukovina was extracted from the Porte, though this had nothing to do with the Polish partitions.) Austria's subsequent gains, West Galicia and Cracow, were made in the third partition of 1795 and were to prove transitory, for by the terms of the treaty of Schönbrunn Napoleon annexed these to the Grand Duchy of Warsaw and then by the terms of the Vienna Settlement Austria had to submit to the inclusion of West Galicia in the new Russian dominated Kingdom of Poland, though she was granted a share in the supervision of Cracow, which was made a Free City and which she ultimately annexed in 1846 after an unsuccessful revolt had taken place there (p. 148).

Galicia was in a very backward condition and the Bukovina even more so when Austria took them over in the 1770s. The economy was, of course, almost exclusively agricultural, though there were a small number of industrial ventures underway, generally concerned with the preparation of flax. In the eastern half of the province especially the condition of the peasants was deplorable. In the Bukovina it was even worse. Feudal obligations were often extreme by the standards of the other Habsburg dominions and knowledge of farming methods and the nature of farming implements were primitive. To the west, conditions were rather better and it was here that the economy was most developed, but the once profitable export trade in wheat had declined by seventy-five per cent in the two hundred years prior to Austrian annexation and was to suffer further in the period following the Vienna settlement as a result of Prussian tariff policies.

In social structure Galicia had most in common with Hungary, having a disproportionately high noble population, the vast majority of whom were 'small' or 'sandalled' nobility, either altogether landless or farmers of very moderate means indeed. Such middle class as there was was mainly made up of Jews, who comprised rather less than eight per cent of the total population.

As was the case in Bohemia and in Hungary, there was considerable racial diversity in Galicia. The western half of the province was predominantly Polish: in the east the majority were Ruthenes, though there were significant Polish enclaves here too: and in the Bukovina the northern half was Ukrainian and the southern Roumanian. This racial diversity, combined with peasant resentment of landlords' harshness, was to serve the Habsburgs well as they sought to re-establish control after the Napoleonic wars.

During the Napoleonic period the Polish elements in Galicia had tended to sympathise with the French in the dubious hope that Napoleon would restore the Polish kingdom and give it back its former significance. In the disillusionment that followed Napoleon's collapse the Austrian authorities feared that the Poles of Galicia might transfer their hopes to Russia, the more so since Alexander was toying with the possibilities of a liberal approach to the newly constituted Kingdom of Poland in the years immediately after the signing of the Vienna settlement. A bid was therefore made for Polish support. In 1817 the province of Galicia was styled a 'Kingdom', it was given its own Viceroy and, briefly, its own Chancellery in Vienna, and Metternich's philosophy of cultivating the Provincial Estates was put into practice when the Galician Diet was summoned for the first time in thirty-five years.

However, there was not enough in these measures to win over the Polish nobility, the majority of whom remained sullen and resentful, the more so since the officials attendant on the Viceroy were almost exclusively German. Nonetheless, when the 1830 revolt against Russia flared up in the Kingdom of Poland, Galicia remained quiet, and when an attempt was made to raise Galicia in 1833 it was easily put down. This relative stability of Galicia was perhaps misleading, however, for a number of the Polish nobility were engaged in a waiting game under the direction of an émigré committee in Paris.

The abortive revolt of 1846

To be effective any rising in Galicia would need peasant support and after much conflict the nobles were persuaded by the more progressive amongst them to make a bid for peasant sympathy. In 1845 the Galician Diet petitioned Vienna for a programme whereby remaining feudal obligations would be lifted and the peasants would be able to buy their own lands over a period of years, whilst the government would facilitate the deal by compensating the nobility. The Paris committee then proceeded to plan revolt on the assumption that the support of the peasants was now assured. Fortunately for the Austrians, however, this was not so and when the revolt broke out in February 1846 the peasants proved more eager for their land than hostile to the

Habsburgs and they turned not on the Austrians but on their landlords, of whom some 1500 were killed or wounded. Thus the Habsburgs reaped some recompense for the work that government officials had done in reducing the harshness of peasant conditions on many noble estates.

The annexation of Cracow

Meanwhile a simultaneous revolt in Cracow lasted only slightly longer, being effectively subdued as first Austrian, then Russian and finally Prussian troops marched in. Thus peace was restored and the Austrian position not only confirmed but apparently consolidated when in November 1847 Russia and Prussia agreed, reluctantly it must be admitted, to her annexation of Cracow as a precaution against further unrest there.

The annexation of Cracow was, however, something of an embarrassment as far as Metternich was concerned, for he was immediately subjected to a stream of abuse from hostile critics such as Palmerston, who angrily accused him of forsaking the carefully structured balance of the Vienna settlement to satisfy the acquisitive instincts of Austria. In fact Metternich's motives were surely defensive. In Cracow he saw nothing but a centre for ambitious and hot-headed extremists and he thus regarded the annexation as a 'police measure'. For him the agitation of the Polish question was the work of selfish and irresponsible men: 'the enthusiasm for "Poland" is only a formula to cloak what hides behind it – the Revolution in its most brutal form'. His heroes were rather the common people, who 'understand that they can be Polish without having a Polish government'.

Meanwhile there were a number of frictious issues still to be faced. First of all, the annexation of Cracow altered considerably the ratio of Poles to other nationalities in the area and amongst the Poles of Cracow there were many who were strongly committed to the nationalist idea, whilst in Galicia itself the Polish nobility were bitterly resentful of the peasants' assault on their fellow nobles in 1846 and were inclined to see in the massacres some kind of ingenious Austrian plot. Furthermore the peasants themselves posed a serious problem. There was widespread expectation that the Habsburg government would now give the peasants their liberty, a thing that Metternich in particular was unwilling to do for fear of offending the Tsar, and on top of this, peasant dissatisfaction was further intensified by a series of natural calamities – disastrous floods in the Vistula basin destroyed homes, crops and cattle and in the consequent starvation situation an epidemic of hunger typhus took further toll. The Austrian response, two compromise Patents of April and November 1847 extending the peasants' right of appeal and reducing the robot to the Bohemian level together with a stepping up of the Austrian garrisons in Galicia and Cracow, did nothing to relieve the tension.

1848

As news of revolt elsewhere penetrated Galicia it was only to be expected that the initiative would be taken up once more. Both in Cracow and in Lemburg deputations petitioned the Austrian authorities for concessions – the release of political prisoners, the formation of national guards, the abolition of the robot, the introduction of Polish as the language of administration and so on. Representatives of the two cities then went on to Vienna, where they combined to demand the right to reorganise Galicia on a national basis.

In this situation the Habsburgs had two advantages, the skill of Francis Stadion the acting Viceroy in Galicia and the fact that there was an increasing determination amongst the Ruthenian population to resist the Polish bid for supremacy in Galicia. The Ruthenians were generally ignored by the Polish activists and thus they tended to look to Austria for support. Stadion put the situation to good use, encouraging the Ruthenes to form their own Rada (assembly) and to stake out a positive claim for consideration. Meanwhile he was also able to deprive the Poles of the initiative over the issue of feudal obligations, for on 26 April 1848 he received authority from the government in Vienna to announce the termination of feudal dues and to promise compensation to the landowners. Thus, thwarted by a combination of good sense in Galicia itself and prevarication in Vienna, where firm assurances on the future of Galicia were not forthcoming, the Poles lost much of their impetus until finally, in November 1848, the extremists were driven into attempting a desperate coup in Lemburg only to be conclusively defeated by Austrian troops under General von Hammerstein.

In Galicia at least the Habsburgs emerged from 1848 relatively secure, for their handling of the Ruthenian and peasant issues, erratic though it had been, had successfully outmanoeuvred the more extreme champions of purely Polish interests. Resentful though the Polish nobility were to remain, they did not commit themselves to action when, in 1863, their compatriots in the Kingdom of Poland erupted once again against the weight of Russian rule.

[24] ITALY

The Habsburgs emerged from the Congress of Vienna as the dominant power in Italy. With Lombardy–Venetia under the direct rule of the Emperor, and Parma, Modena and Tuscany each ruled by a member of the Habsburg family, the dynasty was better placed in Italy then ever before. Some, notably the Archduke John, criticised the assumption of such a responsibility in Italy on the grounds that the Habsburgs should be concentrating their energics on Germany, but Metternich was convinced that the Habsburgs had a role to play in Italy that was vital not only to their own interests but also to those of Europe as a whole.

Italy, he argued, was not 'naturally' suited to unity. All her traditions were provincial, not national. Of the Italians themselves he commented, 'hating each other, their only real patriotism hardly extends beyond the province or town in which they first saw light of day'. Thus it followed, Metternich believed, that

if Italy were to be saved from anarchy there must be order imposed from outside and Austria was the logical power to supply
this, as neither of the other two powers whose geographical position might commend them was suited to the task – France because there could be no question of extending her influence after
recent experiences and Spain because she was herself so unstable.

Believing that nationalist ideas on the future of Italy were
fundamentally illusory, a view with which incidentally many
intelligent Italians agreed, Metternich determined to suppress
such dangerous thinking. Further, he intended to deal firmly
with radical thinking in general in conformity with his conviction
that what was needed was a quarantine period for the exter-
mination of the unsettling ideas of the Revolution. This policy
he would implement directly in Lombardy–Venetia, by strong
advice in the other Habsburg states and, he hoped, by persuasion
in the territories that were not under Habsburg rule, the Papal
States, Piedmont, Naples and Sicily.

Metternich's policy of repression

His initial success in converting the non-Habsburg rulers of Italy
to his way of thinking is strikingly evidenced by the fact that
Austrian troops intervened by invitation to counter revolts in
Naples and Piedmont in 1821 and in the Papal States on a number of occasions after 1830. Less encouraging from Metternich's
point of view, however, was the fact that he had also to intervene
on behalf of the Habsburg rulers of Modena and Parma in 1831
and that the France of Louis-Philippe began to challenge the
right of Austria to determine the future of Italy single-handed
with the launching of the Ancona expedition in 1832 (p. 97).
For all this Metternich never wavered in his determination to
defend conservative principles in Italy. His constant vigilance
and his energy behind the scenes were truly incredible and the
lengths to which he was prepared to go are nowhere better
evidenced than in a letter of 1831 which he wrote to the Imperial
ambassador in Rome, taking the further precaution what is more
of forwarding copies to Naples, Parma, Florence and Turin. The

problem that inspired the letter was apparently a slight one, but to Metternich it was too dangerous to ignore. There was, he had learned, a disciple of the doctrines of Saint-Simon at the French Academy in Rome and as the carrier of such ideas he must be carefully watched. The disciple was, in fact, none other than the French composer Hector Berlioz, who would undoubtedly have been hugely flattered had he known of the stir that his presence had caused, for Metternich's instructions to the ambassador were comprehensive to say the least:

you will doubtless feel it wise to inform the papal government of the nature of the views with which the young man appears to be imbued, also to warn and give salutary advice to those young artists who are now living in Rome and are also subjects of the Emperor against the troublesome influence of this contact. If Monsieur Berlioz, when leaving Rome, comes to the Imperial Embassy for a visa to enter the Austrian territories, Your Excellency will refuse one in this case.

Conciliatory aims

The repression of dangerous ideas was thus an axiomatic part of Metternich's policies in Italy as it was of his policies elsewhere, but repression was by no means the sum total of what he proposed. Indeed he planned to make repression more or less unnecessary in time, for he hoped to win the Italian states to a willing acceptance of the role of Austria in their midst. With this end in view he sought to make Habsburg government in Italy the sort of government that he believed most thinking Italians wanted and he sought to commend Austrian authority yet further by developing an economic relationship between Austria and the various states which would be mutually beneficial.

In theory his approach to the problem of how best to govern Lombardy–Venetia was both generous and sensitive, as can be seen in a memorandum on the subject that he submitted to the Emperor Francis in 1817 and it is worth looking at this in some detail, for it is so tragically at odds with what actually happened and it does show a side of Metternich that does not often emerge:

It cannot be unknown to your Majesty that the tedious programme
of business, the design attributed to your Majesty of wishing to give
an entirely German character to the Italian provinces, the com-
position of the courts, where the Italians daily see with sorrow German
magistrates appointed to office, and the prolongation of the contro-
versies between the Vienna court and the Holy See, are the main
causes to which discontent is ascribed. Since these causes seem to me
to be all more or less of a kind capable of removal, and since the
paternal views of your Majesty have in this respect long been known
to me, I think it is my duty to repeat again, with the greatest respect,
how important it would be, from a political point of view, to remove
as soon as possible these defects and shortcomings of the administration in this most interesting part of the monarchy, to quicken
and advance the progress of business, to conciliate the national spirit
and self-love of the nation by giving to these provinces a form of constitution which might prove to the Italians that we have no desire
to deal with them exactly as with the German provinces of the
monarchy, or, so to speak, to weld them with these provinces; that
we should there appoint, and especially in the magisterial offices, able
natives of the country, and that, above all, an endeavour should be
made to unite more closely with ourselves the clergy and the class of
writers who have most influence on public opinion. I do not doubt
that it is possible to gain this most desirable and beneficial end without encountering great difficulties, and even without being exposed
to the necessity of departing from those general principles upon
which the administration of the other parts of the monarchy is based
– principles which unquestionably must be preserved in the interests
of the common weal, though their application may admit of many
modifications. I cherish, lastly, the hope that whenever your Majesty
is induced to set in motion the salutary designs long contemplated
and to establish the well-being of these provinces on an enduring
basis, public opinion will declare itself for Austria, discontent will
disappear with its causes, and the Italians will at last regard Austria
as the only government which can afford a sure support to public
tranquillity. If ever this day should come, then the influence of
foreigners will cease to be feared and we shall gain an influence far
more effective – the influence granted by opinion.

This memorandum, together with one submitted in 1841 on
the desirability of developing economic links, represents the

creative aspect of Metternich's approach to Italy. The tragedy, from his point of view, was that in practice the Habsburgs failed to convince Italian opinion that they really had any creative plans at all. The mood of the 1817 memorandum was never implemented, for the Emperor paid it scant attention and the picture that predominated in Lombardy–Venetia, despite the fact that the Austrian government there was probably the best in Italy, was one of oppression. The banning of Confalonieri's liberal newspaper, the *Conciliatore*, in 1818 and the eventual imprisonment of Confalonieri himself and of others such as Silvio Pellico had more impact on popular opinion than the un-implemented good intentions of the Austrian Chancellor. As for the economic programme it was probably projected too late any-way, for by the forties the force of criticism was perhaps beyond the reach of such slow-working manoeuvres.

Metternich loses control

The truth of the matter was that the Austrians never succeeded in giving any convincing demonstration of constructive intent. This was fatal, for without such a demonstration how could the dreary round of repression be justified? As it was the Austrians squandered what advantages they had and these were really quite considerable. Their greatest chance, as Metternich saw quite clearly at an early stage, lay in the opposition's lack of unanimity. In the years following the overthrow of Napoleon, secret societies proliferated in Italy (a police report of 1822–3 listed over fifty, ranging from the well-known Carbonari in the south down to such lesser known but intriguingly named organis-ations as the *Spillo Nero* – the 'Black Pin' – in the Papal States), but their mutual hostility more or less nullified their effectiveness. Similarly in the realms of more abstract political thinking there was little agreement. Many held strong views on the future of Italy, Gioberti, Mazzini, Balbo and so on, but there was endless disagreement on detail. Was the end to be pursued a national Republic, a loosely knit federal state, or what, and who was to provide the leadership, the Pope, the King of Sardinia or the people?

Had Austria been able to project a constructive image, these scattered forces might conceivably have caused her but little inconvenience, but because she could not the forces of opposition almost imperceptibly drew together, temporarily at least, submerging their differences in making common cause against Austria, which became a welcome focus for discontent. From this moment Metternich was lost, for his only response to criticism of a subversive nature was repression of a more obdurate kind. The more the opposition railed at him, the meaner he became and the more intense the overall situation. In the last resort he knew of only one solution in circumstances such as these. As he put it in a letter to the Grand Duke of Tuscany in April 1847, 'how can one combat the evil? There is only one way and that is to *govern*'.

By the late forties Metternich was in a hopeless corner. His grip on Piedmont was disintegrating fast, as Charles Albert abandoned the Austrian alliance and began to develop an individual line of his own and the situation in the Papal States took an alarming change for the worse, when, in 1846, the election of a reputedly liberal pope, Pius IX, instilled new arrogance into the forces of disorder, an arrogance that was in no way diminished by Metternich's high-handed military occupation of the papal city of Ferrara in July 1847, despite protests from the pope himself. But the key to it all lay further back, in his failure to implement constructive government in the North of Italy, for this had made of Austria such a repressive figurehead as to give the forces of opposition in Italy an appearance of harmony and unanimity whose artificiality could only be exposed by his fall. The speed with which that apparent unanimity did disintegrate after his fall only serves further to emphasise the most ironic point of all – that he was right in believing that Italy was not ready for unity and that had his policies in practice measured up to his politics on paper Italy at least might have been spared a revolution in 1848.

Austria's position with regard to Germany was a delicate one.
Her nominal leadership in German affairs, long implicit in the
Habsburg monopoly of the Imperial Crown, was recognised
again in her presidency of the new German Confederation, but if
her leadership were to be anything more than nominal she would
need to be a persuasive president, for there were forces stirring
in the Germany of 1815 which were not altogether in harmony
with Habsburg interests.

Metternich's attitude to Germany was much the same as his
attitude to Italy. He did not believe that she was historically
suited to unity. 'German patriotism is directed towards a variety
of objects. Ever since the common fatherland came into being
there have been quite distinct public trends. Provincial patriotism is the one to which the German is most accessible', he wrote,
and indeed he believed that the component parts of Prussia were
too diversified to allow of her becoming a really great power, let
alone the whole of Germany managing to do so. Thus the ideal
solution, both for the German states and for Europe, was a con-
federate structure in which Austria would keep a benevolent
watch on the rights and interests of all.

Such an argument was to come under pressure on two counts.
There developed during the period 1815–48 two distinct schools
of thought on the German problem, neither of which was acceptable to Metternich. The first was the so-called kleindeutsch or
little-German school, which looked to exclude Austria from
German affairs and to build a state which would thus almost
certainly be dominated by Prussia. Metternich could see nothing
but folly in this:

I am convinced that Austria alone serves the true interests of Germany and would be able to maintain her domestic peace – and that
without any ulterior motives. This can best be understood by reference to the facts: the size of our empire, as a political unit, has reached
saturation point: we have nothing to demand of Germany except her
own tranquillity. Prussia, on the other hand, has an urge to expan-

ion which could only be satisfied to the detriment of other German states.

The alternative view was the grossdeutsch or large-German concept, that Austria was the natural leader of Germany and should continue to be so; but this too was a philosophy fraught with danger from the Austrian point of view, for it tended to carry the implication that Austria's prime responsibility was towards Germany and that she should reduce her commitments elsewhere accordingly. Thus Metternich preferred to discourage dynamic thinking on the future of Germany and to maintain the relatively ineffectual organisation of 1815.

If he were to succeed in this he would have to prevail against radicalism in the German states and in particular he would have to convince the king of Prussia of the folly of encouraging any challenge to the existing structure. In both these projects he was, in fact, relatively successful.

Militant patriotic feeling

In the years immediately following the defeat of Napoleon, German radicalism appeared to Metternich to be a real threat. Considerable, if confused, enthusiasm had been generated in 1813–14 and a militant patriotism was in the air. Often this patriotism was no more than the provincial state patriotism that Metternich had noted as being a divisive rather than a unifying force, but in some cases there was a mounting enthusiasm for 'Germany' as a nation and a real urge for change, in which a wild hotchpotch of liberal slogans was enthusiastically manipulated. Particularly susceptible to such ideas were the students and indeed two of the major heroes of the movement were actually university teachers, Arndt and Fichte. Of a more practical bent was another powerful propagator of the German idea, Father Jahn.

Jahn's utterances had a peculiarly crude and subversive flavour and they provide an interesting preview of some of the worst excesses of the twentieth century – 'Germany needs a war of her own in order to feel her power; she needs a feud with Frenchdom in order to develop her national way of life in all its fullness';

and then 'the father who lets his daughter learn French is no
better than the man who apprentices his daughter to whoredom'
But perhaps Jahn's greatest contribution was as an organiser
The years immediately following 1814 witnessed a tremendou
growth of youth organisations, in particular his own gymnasti
societies or *Turnerschaften* and the popular student societie
known as *Burschenschaften*. Obsessed with a confusion of libera
and nationalist doctrines, these organisations were anathema to
Metternich, but there was little that he could do about it a
first, for a number of German rulers were themselves encouraging
liberal ideas in their own territories. Indeed insanity reache
something of a peak to Metternich's mind when the Grand Duke
of Weimar actually encouraged a student gathering to celebrate
the three hundredth anniversary of the Lutheran Reformation
on a day which also happened (significantly) to be the anniver
sary of the battle of Leipsig. This Wartburg Fest, held on 18–19
October 1817, proved something of a Jacobin orgy with furious
denunciations of the Vienna settlement and of conservatism in
general and a ritualistic burning of offending texts. The last
straw came when the priest of the Lutheran church at Eisenach
agreed to round off the proceedings by administering the com-
munion to all the students involved.

At this stage Metternich was at his wit's end, for not even
Frederick William III of Prussia seemed reliable on the maintenance of conservative principles. However, the student movement more or less destroyed itself when the murder of Kotzebue
in 1819 gave Metternich the opportunity to convince the rulers
of Germany of the folly of their ways and to manoeuvre them
into unanimous acceptance of the Carlsbad Decrees (pp. 112–
114). Thereafter the radical pressure on authority diminished
rapidly in Germany and when the Paris revolution of 1830
brought with it minor repercussions in Germany including another student uproar, this time the Hambach Fest of May 1832,
Metternich was able to rush through the Diet of the Confederation further repressive legislation, the Six Articles, which were
unanimously approved in July of that year. Political associations
and public festivals were now prohibited and the right of the

Confederation to intervene in its corporate capacity in the event of any member sovereign granting constitutional concessions to his subjects or having the same extorted from him was affirmed.

Of considerable significance in the success of Metternich in keeping the Diet loyal to conservative principles was the attitude of Prussia, for Metternich was able from the murder of Kotzebue onwards to prevail upon Frederick William III to put the considerable influence of his state behind the conservative drive. As he remarked with satisfaction in 1832,

the mental superiority that we enjoy over the Prussian government is so decisive that I have yet to see that government fail to go back on what it has only too often advanced with great rapidity and frivolity, once it is sure that our point of view differs from its own.

This was a major success, for the proponents of a kleindeutsch Germany would make little headway whilst the natural leader of such a movement was in Austria's pocket.

The succession of Frederick William IV in 1840 looked ominous for a while, for he started off in generous mood, freeing Jahn from the rigours of police supervision and allowing the veteran Arndt to lecture once again at the university in Bonn. However, it soon became clear that such projects for change as he did envisage were not of a liberal nature and that his benevolent approach was a byproduct of his romantic vision of the king as a paternal figure of medieval style rather than of any truly progressive convictions. Metternich thus had little to fear from the new king, save perhaps his mercurial temperament which was to lapse eventually into madness in the late 1850s, and whilst Prussia remained firmly committed to conservative principles it was a reasonable supposition that radicalism in Germany might be held at bay.

The Zollverein

The apparent success of Metternich in convincing the German rulers of the wisdom of repressing radical thinking was, however, being quietly but effectively undermined by economic developments in Germany, as Metternich himself came to see all too

clearly. His whole approach to Germany was based on his confidence that the particularism of the various states would militate
against any projects for unity, since such projects would inevitably involve the surrender of a measure of provincial independence. Yet while this was true on the political level, economic
pressures were working in the opposite direction. In 1818 Prussia
made herself into a free trade area and the years that followed
saw, after an initial reluctance, a spate of free trade agreements
with other states, so much so that in January 1834 there was
established the Zollverein, a free trade organisation involving
eighteen north German states and eager to incorporate more.
Rival organisations in central and southern Germany were subsequently engulfed and the one major outsider by 1848 was
Austria, a situation of dire significance to Austria's desire to remain dominant in Germany. As Metternich pointed out in 1841,
'Austria is on the point of seeing herself to a certain extent
excluded from the rest of Germany . . . and treated as a foreign
country'.

To do Metternich justice he had pressed for the acceptance of
invitations to join the Zollverein both in 1834 and again in 1841,
but in both cases industrialist scruples about the tariff revisions
involved had defeated him and his alternative plans for the
capturing of south German trade by building railway links with
the Adriatic and the Mediterranean proved ineffectual.

The depressing truth was that whilst Metternich had managed
to maintain the conservatism of the German rulers to a considerable extent, he was unable to prevent, or even to become a
shareholder in an economic movement which was in direct opposition to the tradition of particularism in Germany on which all
his calculations were based. The events of 1848–9 showed that
the will of the rulers was still the decisive factor in German politics and to an extent the refusal of the German crown by
Frederick William IV in 1849 was a belated tribute to Metternich's achievement in Germany, but how long the German rulers
could continue to resist the underlying forces of change was far
from certain, for Metternich had not been able to arrest the
progress of such forces.

The years immediately preceding 1848 saw a steady growth of unrest in the Habsburg lands. The Galician troubles of 1846 were but a foretaste of worse to come, for in Austria, in Bohemia, in Hungary, in Italy and in many of the German states there was a mounting demand for liberal reforms and the advent of economic strain, with the poor harvests of 1846–7 and the credit crisis of 1847, made the situation still more critical. As dissatisfaction mounted the name of Metternich became symbolic of all that was wrong. There developed a naïve assumption that it was the repressive Chancellor alone who stood between the subjects of the Habsburgs and fulfilment and so it was that Metternich's resignation on 13 March 1848 served as a catalyst, unleashing the forces of revolt that had been so long pent up.

The vital pressure was applied by the Viennese. Knowledge of the acutely dangerous situation in Italy (Radetzky had imposed martial law in Lombardy–Venetia on 22 February), and of liberal agitation in Germany, combined with news of the Paris revolution and of Kossuth's challenging speech to the Lower House of the Hungarian Diet on 3 March, led many responsible citizens to fear that Metternich was about to embark on yet another expensive campaign of repression, which would surely lead to a serious financial crisis and an epidemic of inflation. Thus bourgeois interests tended momentarily to yield to the mood of the more radical students who were vociferously demanding the resignation of Metternich. The situation was further complicated by outbursts of working class violence and the position was stated in the baldest terms when, at about seven o'clock on the evening of 13 March, representatives of the Civic Guard announced that they could not guarantee order unless three conditions were met: the troops must be withdrawn from the city, the students armed and Metternich dismissed.

Even this was not the end, for Metternich was strongly supported by Windisch-Graetz, who was subsequently to emerge as one of the ogres of the military repression, but Ferdinand and

Ludwig were eventually swayed by the counsels of the Archduke John and Kolowrat, who could hardly be expected to miss such an opportunity of exacting their revenge on Metternich, whose fate was finally sealed by Ferdinand in words of shattering simplicity. 'After all, I am the sovereign', he remarked, 'and the decision lies with me. Tell the people I agree to everything.'

Metternich's flight

And so it was that Metternich was forced at last to leave the stage. Habsburg meanness had never been more strongly in evidence, for the old man who had served the dynasty for so long was given no assistance. In ready cash he had only five hundred florins in paper money (all his property in Austria and Bohemia was shortly to be sequestered by the new Diet) and this deficiency was only remedied by the generosity of personal friends, notably Baron Hügel, who played a major role in the escape, and Baron Rothschild. With his wife Melanie the seventy-five-year-old chancellor was spirited out of a gate by night and driven to the Liechtenstein estate at Feldsburg. From there the party were moved on by order of the local burgomaster, who would not take responsibility for so unpopular a visitor. There then began a long and arduous journey by road and rail in which all manner of discomfort and grotesque precautions had to be endured. Disguises and false passports abounded as hostile terri-tory was slowly traversed and it was not until they reached Arnheim in Holland that they could afford to relax a little, eventually making the sea crossing to England and arriving in London on 19 April.

Meanwhile, the news of Metternich's fall brought jubilation and frenzied activity. On 17 March Ferdinand accepted the idea of radical reform for Hungary. On 18 March fighting broke out in Lombardy–Venetia and, as Radetzky withdrew his troops to the Quadrilateral, Venice declared itself a republic on 21 March and Milan announced a provisional government on the twenty-third. A deputation from Bohemia arrived in Vienna on 20 March and in Germany a major breakthrough seemed to have been achieved when an insurrection in Berlin on 18 March drove Frederick William into a flurry of constitutional concession, which was promptly taken up by other German rulers. Meanwhile in Vienna itself the government announced its intention on 15 March of summoning a Diet to discuss a new constitution.

For a moment it really looked as though it had been one man alone who had stood between the Habsburg provinces and reform and that now at last a major rethinking of Habsburg policies was to follow. And yet the recipe concocted by Metternich's successors was no more generous than his own as it turned out. By 1850 the revolution had been bloodily suppressed in Italy, Hungary and Bohemia, and even, though with much less bloodshed, in Austria itself. The constitutional concessions of 1848 were soon modified to suit the requirements of a government that was quite as authoritarian as its predecessors and rather more energetic as well. The truth of the matter was that by 1848 the Habsburg Empire of the Vienna settlement was under such pressure that to make concessions, in some areas at least, was to surrender. Either the heirs of Metternich had to stick grimly to the policies of repression or they must rethink the Habsburg role, renounce the Vienna structure and build again on a somewhat different basis. In 1850 they chose the former path, though by 1870 they had been forced onto the latter.

For Metternich himself, of course, there could be no question of alternatives, for he believed in the Vienna structure as crucial both to Habsburg interests and to European stability. But one cannot but wonder whether by a more vigorous policy of constructive concession earlier on he might not have saved himself from the vicious circle in which he ultimately found himself, a circle in which criticism and repression agitated one another progressively to further extremes until the fatal point of no return was reached, the point where concession could be interpreted only as surrender and no longer as an act of magnanimity or constructive inspiration.

Principal Events, 1848–9

AN OUTLINE OF THE RISE AND FALL OF REVOLUTIONARY FORTUNES IN THE HABSBURG LANDS

AUSTRIA	HUNGARY	BOHEMIA	GALICIA	LOMBARDY–VENETIA
1848				
	3 March. Kossuth's speech in the Lower House of the Hungarian Diet demands a new constitution for Hungary and similar concessions elsewhere in the Habsburg Lands			
13 March. Resignation of Metternich 15 March. The Emperor announces his intention of calling a Constitutional Assembly (Reichstag), in which all the Provincial Estates are to be represented and in which there is to be increased burgher representation	17 March. The Emperor grants a measure of independence to the Hungarian Estates on the basis of which they draft a new constitutional formula the 'April Laws'	March. Various demands drawn up in Prague and submitted to Vienna (Czech interests predominate over German, Moravian, etc)	March. Deputations from Lemburg and Cracow go to Vienna, but get no firm reply	

21 March. Venice proclaims herself a Republic
23 March. Milan announces a Provisional Government
Charles Albert of Piedmont enters Lombardy to assist her in her struggle against the Austrians

28 March. Imperial plan for the abolition of the robot and for landlord compensation announced

8 April. Limited concessions made by the Emperor – the 'Bohemian Charter'

25-26 April. Attempted rising in Cracow subdued by Austrian troops

11 May. Popular, pressure forces the government to allow a popular suffrage in the election of the Reichstag

1 June. Palacky's 'Slav Congress' congregates in Prague: viewed with great suspicion by the German population there

AUSTRIA	HUNGARY	BOHEMIA	GALICIA	LOMBARDY–VENETIA
		12 June. Windisch-Graetz takes advantage of unrest, both racial and economic, to take over the city of Prague		25 July. Radetzky defeats the Piedmontese at Custozza. 8 August. Charles Albert signs an armistice
	June/July. Vienna encourages Croat/Serb opposition to the Magyar programme			
October. Mounting popular unrest in Vienna over unemployment and in sympathy with the revolution in Hungary. The refusal of a regiment to entrain for Hungary and the murder of a government minister, Latour, give Windisch-Graetz the excuse to storm the city, which falls on 30 October	3 October. The Emperor orders the dissolution of the Hungarian Diet and proclaims Jellačić, the Croat leader, the 'Representative of the Crown in Hungary'. Prolonged fighting follows		2 November. Lemburg rising quashed by Hammerstein	

2 December. The abdication of Ferdinand and the accession of Franz Joseph reflect a steady restoration of authority

1849

2 March. Completion of the Reichstag's draft constitution
4 March. Reichstag dissolved, its constitution declared obsolescent and a constitution drafted by the government promulgated in its stead

June. Russia agrees to send troops to assist the Austrians

August. Capitulation of the main Hungarian forces

31 March. Charles Albert renews hostilities
23 March. Radetzky defeats the Piedmontese at Novara. Charles Albert abdicates

6 August. Lombardy resumes peaceful relations with Austria
22 August. Venice capitulates

PART VI
The Problem of Interpretation

[27] THE HISTORIANS

It is far from easy to produce a balanced assessment of Metternich for he has drawn from historians the most varied reactions. Few if any would deny that Metternich was a failure, but within that consensus there is room for a wide diversity of emphasis. For some he was the villain of the piece and for others his was a failure of the noblest kind, while many more have both good and bad to say of him. The object of the pages that follow is to trace some broad trends of opinion and the very fact that certain historians will be quoted under more than one heading should emphasise the fact that there is no clear cut solution to the problem of interpretation.

Since Metternich's policies involved as a prerequisite to any constructive activity the relentless reduction of the proponents of the twin 'heresies' of liberalism and nationalism, it is not to be wondered at that his most vehement critics have been historians dedicated to these self-same 'heresies'.

In the eyes of German historians of the late nineteenth and early twentieth centuries for example Metternich had played a truly diabolical role in arresting the exciting growth of German nationality, so promising during the years leading up to the overthrow of Napoleon and so viciously cut back thereafter. In the interests of the anachronistic Habsburg Empire Metternich had set himself against progress and to historians such as Treitschke the eventual turning of the tables in the Prussian defeat of Austria at Königgrätz in 1866 was just, if long overdue, deserts for the Habsburg dynasty's persistent obstruction of the 'dynamic forces of history' from 1815.

Treitschke in fact put the main blame on to the emperor Francis and demoted Metternich to an utterly subordinate position as no more than Francis's agent. This line was further developed by Metternich's most malevolent critic of the twentieth century, Viktor Bibl, who gave the argument a sinister twist with the suggestion that Metternich knew full well that his policies would be disastrous for the Habsburg empire but carried them out nonetheless in order to satisfy his master and thus safeguard his job. Bibl's assault on Metternich, in fact, is even more dramatic than Treitschke's because it is more comprehensive. Whereas Treitschke's grievance was a straightforward case of frustrated national pride, Bibl's is more complex. His sympathies are largely with Austria whose true interests he accuses Metternich of having betrayed. As a liberal Bibl totally rejects Metternich's 'principles' and moves on to a number of controversial conclusions, among them that Metternich was, through his own short-sightedness, entirely responsible for the March Revolution of 1848, that his mistaken policies in Germany and Italy led to the subsequent Austrian disasters of Solferino and Königgrätz and finally that 'the much delayed opening of the Eastern Question, which he did not want touched, led to the world war'. Small wonder then that Bibl entitled his most scathing work *Metternich, der Dämon Österreichs* (*Metternich, Austria's Evil Genius*). No one has quite matched the sustained hostility of his analysis.

For the majority of historians, however, such an extreme position is not acceptable. Indeed most take it for granted that some sort of conservative policy was to be expected in the circumstances in 1815. What provokes criticism is not so much that Metternich's course was conservative as that it was conservative in a sterile rather than in a dynamic way. What happened to the creative confidence of the Political Testament that Metternich had addressed to Alexander in 1820?

The Governments, in establishing the principle of stability, will in no wise exclude the development of what is good, for stability is not immobility.

It is Metternich's failure to live up to this declaration that upsets some of his more sympathetic interpreters, notably Heinrich von Srbik, Metternich's most comprehensive biographer, who argues that in the conservatism that Metternich evolved the repressive more or less came to exclude the creative:

He often endeavoured to maintain what was ripe for destruction in the old conditions and to suppress what was fresh with life and striving towards the sun in the new, and he only looked upon as positive what had become, not what was in the process of becoming . . . he, the last great master of the doctrine of balance, was unable to find the balance between preserving and developing which is the deepest meaning of conservatism.

Very closely tied in with this disappointment at the essential bankruptcy of Metternich's approach is the reproach that he gave up too easily. Admittedly the problems facing him were enormous and yet it is surely out of great problems that great solutions grow. There is little nobility in Metternich's attempts at self-justification after his fall:

Let anyone look at the situations confronting Austria and all of Europe between 1809 and 1848 and let him ask himself whether any one man's insight could have worked a cure. I claim to have recognised the situation but I admit to my inability to erect a new structure in our Empire and in Germany; that is why I have dedicated myself to the preservation of that which was already in existence.

It is on this rather plaintive and feeble approach that a number of historians have focused to good effect, amongst them Professor Henry A. Kissinger:

Those statesmen who have achieved final greatness did not do so through resignation, however well founded. It was given to them not only to maintain the perfection of order, but to have the strength to contemplate chaos, there to find material for fresh creation.

Understanding the situation was not enough. There was a fatal lack of drive in a man who 'for all his belief in his own realism was always ready to mistake a diagnosis for a remedy' (E. L. Woodward). Indeed, as Kissinger points out, the ultimate irony is that Metternich, so much the product of the eighteenth century in his thinking, proved conclusively the fallacy of one of the maxims of the Enlightenment, that knowledge was power.

For such historians as these, generally sympathetic towards Metternich but essentially disappointed in his failure to convert his manifest ability into constructive action, the main superlatives are reserved for his diplomacy. That this was masterly is accepted, but with the crippling reservation that it was essentially barren, an empty tour de force, in that it served only to delay the exposure of the true condition of the Habsburg Empire, for which no life-saving formula had in fact been found. In short, Metternich wins admiration as a manipulator but not as a statesman.

So far then, the picture is not a very impressive one. From the Habsburg point of view Metternich is portrayed as delaying but not averting disaster, whilst from the European point of view his policies are rejected out of hand by the nationalist schools. There is, however, another approach to his policies, one which sets him in a more favourable light. Just as the late nineteenth century was dominated by nationalist enthusiasm and Metternich's views were duly reviled in that climate of opinion, so the twentieth century has witnessed a revulsion against heady nationalism and ruthless *realpolitik* in some quarters. This has produced a climate of opinion less hostile to some of Metternich's views. The champion of the Congress System, the man who spoke in terms of Europe rather than of narrow national priorities, elicits more sympathy perhaps from the twentieth century than from the nineteenth. 'I have for a long time regarded Europe as my homeland', remarked Metternich in 1824 and this idea, coupled with his peace emphasis, has led some to see him as a man ahead of his time rather than behind it.

The most emphatic champion of this theme is Peter Viereck, who finds in Metternich both a sane rejection of demagogic extremism ('Metternich warned against monarchist as well as revolutionary agitators of mob emotion because both produced what he deemed society's greatest danger: fanaticism') and a clearly presented plea for internationalism, which Viereck believes to be the one hope for our future in the twentieth century:

The Metternich demand for a universal law above private force is the last best hope not only of internationalism, not only of peace, but perhaps – since Hiroshima – of the survival of man.

Metternich is in fact incidental to the broader theme of Viereck's work, but other historians dealing exclusively with Metternich have pressed the same general point. E. L. Woodward, by no means a committed enthusiast for Metternich, points out that 'whatever his shortcomings Metternich never thought that the future of civilisation depended on the accentuation of its differences', and Algernon Cecil concludes a sympathetic biography in similar vein. Whilst recognising Metternich's many shortcomings, he maintains that:

It was surely high thinking that caused him to see all local aims in the light of a larger and more lofty purpose; to urge mankind to study to be quiet; to press the nations continually into council, not for the liquidation of war, but, as had hardly been attempted since the days of Constance, for the organisation of peace.

These then are a representative cross-section of assessments of Metternich, some lamenting his failure, others rejoicing at it, but all agreed that from one standpoint or another he was a failure. Even Metternich himself could not have contested this verdict, adept as he was at excusing himself; at best he was a noble failure, for the fact that he extended the life and prestige of the Habsburg Empire beyond the expectations of many and the fact that he did contribute in no small measure to the absence of major European conflict between 1815 and 1848 cannot erase the ultimate truth that he achieved no permanent stability either for the Habsburgs or for Europe. He had set himself a phenomenal task and by his own standards he had failed. It remains to ask the fundamental question, why?

From Metternich's own point of view his failure was easily explicable. He had said all along that there could be no resumption of natural development, that is, right-minded development under the auspices of legitimate authority, unless the Powers first of all combined effectively to exterminate the revolutionary virus. Since that solidarity had not been forthcoming the forces of evil had broken through and the chaos of 1848 came as no surprise to him. Indeed he had virtually resigned himself to disaster as early as 1830 when, disillusioned and shaken by the experience of the Greek war and the revolutions of 1830 itself, he had written so pessimistically to Nesselrode (p. 93). And earlier still, in 1820, he had lamented,

My life has coincided with a hateful time. I have come into the world either too soon or too late; I know that in these years I can accomplish nothing. Earlier I should have had my share of the delights of the period; later I should have taken part in the work of reconstruction; now I spend my time propping up mouldering buildings. I should have been born in 1900 and had the twentieth century before me.

Metternich never abandoned his faith in the rectitude of his own ideas. 'Error has never approached my spirit', he blandly remarked when he met his fellow exile, Guizot, in London in 1848. He simply assumed that the blindness of his contemporaries had led them to a disaster which he could have averted had they been prepared to listen to him. Thus spurned by the present he was left to beg for sympathy from the future:

It may be that someone in the year 2240 will discover my name, and tell the world that in this distant past there was at least one man less limited than the mass of his contemporaries who had pushed fatuity to the point of believing that they had reached the climax of civilisation.

But were Metternich's ideas so right and those that opposed him so false? Only by answering this question can one test the validity of Metternich's rationalisation of disaster.

Essentially Metternich set himself two objectives. The first was to secure peace, stability and prosperity for Europe on the basis of the Vienna equilibrium. The second was to use the breathing space afforded by this period of stability to inject new life into the Habsburg Empire, whose revitalisation Metternich believed to be fundamental to the continuing success of the European balance.

In his approach to European affairs there is much to admire. It has often been said that his avowed concern for the interests of Europe as a whole was no more than a convenient smoke screen to cloud his true priority, which was to preserve intact the Habsburg structure that emerged from the Vienna settlement, but this is less than fair. Metternich was himself very much a European rather than the selfish champion of any particular nationality. He was in a sense a foreigner in Vienna. Certainly he was concerned with the preservation of the Habsburg unit but he was also genuine in his conviction that that unit had a vital role to play in the balance which he believed to be the key to European stability. However, it may be that his concern to satisfy his master led him to saddle the Habsburgs with too much responsibility for their own good.

He was criticised by the Archduke John for having pursued the Italian interest when he should have renounced it in order to concentrate more effectively on Germany, but it is hard to believe that the Emperor Francis could ever have been prevailed upon to accept this. Had he been clairvoyant he might perhaps have allowed Prussia more scope in Germany, perhaps by acceding more fully to her Saxon claims in the Vienna negotiations of 1814–15, in order to concentrate more exclusively on the Panslav elements in the Habsburg territories, for it was in the east that the subsequent outflanking trend in Russian foreign policy was to create such unwelcome pressure later in the century, but again it is hard to believe that the Emperor would have been prepared to sanction such an unorthodox and apparently negative idea. It may be that the balance over which Metternich presided was not the right one, that there was room in it for emergent nationalities and not simply traditional states, but few would deny today that his concern for peace and his concept of stability through balance and regular negotiation had a worthwhile ring to them.

It is in his approach to domestic affairs that he appears most vulnerable. His faith in the natural order as revealed to him, a natural order in which only legitimate authority could take responsibility for change, made demands of such legitimate authority that it simply could not meet. In the last resort the government of which Metternich was a part burned itself out in the attempt to secure his precondition for progress – order, and it never really succeeded in moving into a constructive phase. It was all very well for Metternich to pontificate about government – 'the true merit of a stateman . . . consists in governing so as to avoid a situation where concessions become necessary' – but such a philosophy involves a creative approach to government such as the Habsburg regimes of Francis and Ferdinand conspicuously lacked.

As one surveys Metternich's reform projects and his handling thereof it is hard to resist the conclusion that his genius, if genius it was, was for prevarication rather than for construction. Since the virus of revolution was never adequately conquered one might argue that it was only logical that such attempts at reform as there were were scanty and ineffectual. However, there is a lack of drive about even these few projects that casts significant doubt on Metternich's creative potential. The attempts to get a greater clarification between the executive and advisory functions of government (pp. 115 and 123), the plan to woo the local estates (p. 117), the plan for a central representative body of sorts (pp. 118 and 123), the humane and intelligent memorandum of 1817 on the future of Italy (p. 153), the urge to join the Zollverein (p. 160) – all were blocked. It is surely too glib to place all the blame for this on Francis and the conservatism of the Habsburg bureaucracy. Might not Metternich, in his position of influence with the Emperor, have pressed a little harder? Is there not a suggestion here that Metternich lacked real creative determination, that his unimaginative approach to Hungary and particularly to Széchenyi is the real Metternich and that the handful of reform projects were never founded on any real personal commitment on his part? Such a view certainly finds support in the timidity of an autobiographical memoir in which Metternich looked back on the events of the Vor März period:

the greatest mistake in the Austrian Empire during the period prior to the events of March was the concern of the government with matters that should have been dealt with administratively. This paralysed the machinery of government, overwhelmed the highest levels with trivia and absolved the lowest of all responsibility. *Should I have forced the administration into a different direction? For this I did not have sufficient power. Should I have smashed the machinery? Such a move would only have led to revolution. My task was not to govern nor to administer, but to represent the Empire to foreign countries.*

Still more disquieting is the fact that even if the Powers had been willing to commit themselves effectively to an *alliance solidaire* against the revolutionary trends that Metternich had singled out for annihilation it is hard to believe that they would have got away with it for very long. The natural order that Metternich believed to be the key to stability was increasingly at odds with the social and economic facts of the nineteenth century. From the point of view of Austria and Hungary, as indeed of Russia, it was still realistic to exclude the middle class from political influence for these economies were still so predominantly agrarian. However, in Bohemia, northern Italy and Germany, it was less so and in northern Europe it was out of the question. Furthermore the population trend (the population of Europe almost doubled between 1750 and 1850) was putting an additional strain on traditional social structures and pointing towards the further development of towns and the commercial interests that this implied. Metternich, ever the eighteenth-century aristocrat in his fundamental values, could not have imposed indefinitely an eighteenth-century system in a nineteenth-century context and here perhaps is his greatest limitation – that as the inappropriateness of his concept became increasingly apparent he had no alternative to offer. Rather than adapt to changing circumstances he preferred to go down, clinging to the last to his outmoded principles.

What then is left to say? It is hard to resist the feeling that Metternich's name would have been better served by an earlier death. His cool performance in the difficult years when he took Austria out of Napoleon's grasp and on to the winning side, his successful protection of Habsburg interests as he saw them during the negotiations at Vienna and his consistent championship of the Congress System can scarcely elicit anything but praise from all but the most nationalist interpreters. It is the subsequent failure to build anew, to breathe new life into the Habsburg Empire that disappoints. In a sense he pays the penalty for having gone on too long.

The saviour of the Habsburg Empire, as he must have seemed in 1815, failed to crown that achievement. Admittedly he was by no means in full control of the domestic affairs of the Empire. Admittedly too it may be that the problems of the Empire were insoluble, that a multiracial complex such as this could not long survive the ideologies of post-revolutionary Europe. But even if this was so it is by no means clear that prevarication was the right solution. In the exhaustion of 1815 it probably was, but some new and bold initiative might reasonably have been expected later. It is surely arguable that Metternich's sustained policy of repression made nationalism an uglier force than it might otherwise have been when eventually it did break through. Meanwhile his policy put a crippling and totally negative strain on the Habsburg government and on its finances. If the old order was disintegrating, as Metternich himself confessed in 1830, would it not have been bolder to take the initiative by reducing the area of Habsburg commitment rather than wait to have concessions extorted by force?

In his anticipation of disaster Metternich was half way to facing the facts. As A. J. P. Taylor so succinctly puts it, 'understanding best the Habsburg Empire he despaired of it soonest'. His successors did not even understand the fragility of the situation and by their authoritarian methods they hastened the disintegration that Metternich had staved off for so long. Metternich's perception is undeniable. It is his failure to capitalise on that perception that disappoints. There is something peevishly unsatisfactory about the career of a man whose ultimate response to a black situation is to play for time with ever dwindling confidence rather than seek new ground on which to fight it.

Epilogue

THE LAST YEARS

After the discomforts of the flight from Vienna in March 1848 and the strain of the final years in office Metternich's retirement was in many ways a blissful release. Much as he had enjoyed power and influence it is not unreasonable to suppose that he found the rewards of public office steadily diminishing during the reign of Ferdinand, for there can have been little pleasure in prolonging a situation which could only be 'an agony of uncertain length', if one may transfer Metternich's judgement on the reign of Louis-Philippe to that of his own master.

The Metternichs' main problem during their stay in London was money. Indeed what they would have done but for the generosity of the Tsar, Nicholas, it is impossible to surmise. As it was they spent some time in London (44 Eaton Square), some in Richmond and some in Brighton. Metternich thoroughly enjoyed it, meeting many eminent people and talking over past history and present philosophy with them. The Duke of Wellington was a constant caller, the young Disraeli a fulsome admirer. Even the old enemy, Lord Palmerston, came to call and Metternich also remade the acquaintance of his former mistress, Princess Lieven.

Melanie meanwhile was less content; worried about money and passionately concerned to engineer a return to Vienna (a glorious one at that) she prevailed upon her husband to cross the Channel once more in October 1849, this time to settle in Brussels. Here the impressive sequence of visitors was resumed, with Thiers a notable pilgrim. Then finally came Melanie's great moment. In 1851 Metternich was officially invited back to Vienna and his properties were restored to him. At last, in September, they were there, back in the Rennweg Villa, which had miraculously escaped the attention of the looters.

From then until his death on 11 June 1859 Metternich enjoyed
the prestige of a philosopher king. Among his visitors, either in
Vienna or in one of his country houses, were Frederick William,
Bismarck, Stratford Canning, even an envoy from the Turkish
Sultan and, of course, the Emperor Francis Joseph. How seri-
ously Metternich was taken is another matter. Certainly Francis
Joseph took no notice of his advice not to give Cavour a pretext
for war in 1859.

Fortunately for Metternich he died before the Austrian defeat
at Solferino, though not before the ominous news of Magenta.
Indeed it may well be that as he saw the European peace rent
asunder over the Crimea and the policies of his successors court-
ing disaster in Italy he died as convinced as ever of the right
mindedness of what he had stood for and of the value of what he
had offered to the continent of Europe only to see it rejected and
thrown back in his face. Only a few days before Metternich's
death the writer J. A. Hübner recorded his last interview with
the old man. As Hübner turned to leave, Metternich was rumin-
ating on the past. 'I have been a rock of order', he muttered, 'a
rock of order.'

FURTHER READING

The suggestions below are drawn from the material that is available in English.

Metternich

On Metternich himself there are useful biographies by Algernon Cecil (Eyre and Spottiswoode, 1933), Helen du Coudray (Jonathan Cape, 1935), Constantin de Grünwald (French edition 1939; subsequently published in translation by Falcon books) and Alan Palmer (Weidenfeld and Nicolson, 1972).

There are also useful essays by E. L. Woodward, *Three Studies in European Conservatism* (first published in 1929 and reissued by Cass in 1963), A. J. P. Taylor, *Englishmen and Others* (Hamish Hamilton, 1956) and Sir Lewis Namier *Vanished Supremacies* (first published by Hamish Hamilton in 1958 and re-issued by Peregrine books, 1962). The Woodward is much the longest of the three and contains a useful survey of Metternich's thought as well as his practice. The Taylor is insubstantial but makes its point wittily and the Namier is a masterpiece of concise analysis.

Finally there is a very useful work by G. B. de Sauvigny, *Metternich and his Times* (Darton, Longman and Todd, 1962), a mixture of comment and liberal quotation from Metternich; and also a pamphlet, *Metternich, the Coachman of Europe*, edited by Henry F. Schwarz (published by D. C. Heath and Company, 1965). This consists of a limited cross section of excerpts from various historians and has the advantage that it makes available in translation small fragments from Srbik and Bibl.

The Habsburg Empire

On the Habsburg Empire and its problems the best sources are C. A. Macartney's superb work, *The Habsburg Empire* 1790–1918 (Weidenfeld and Nicolson 1968), the same author's chapters in the *New Cambridge Modern History, volumes nine and ten*, and A. J. P. Taylor's *The Habsburg Monarchy* (first published by Hamish Hamilton in 1948 and re-issued in Peregrine Books, 1964). The latter work is explosive, but thought-provoking on Hungary in 1848.

On the diplomatic history of the period a good guide can be obtained from R. Albrecht-Carrié's *A Diplomatic History of Europe since the Congress of Vienna* (Methuen, 1958). A superb analysis of Metternich's role in the overthrow of Napoleon and in the Congress period is to be found in H. A. Kissinger's *A World Restored* (first published in 1957 by Houghton Mifflin, Boston and re-issued by Universal Library Edition, 1964). This work also contains much sophisticated analysis of Metternich's thought and of the conservative's dilemma. There is a useful chapter on the Congress of Vienna by E. V. Gulick in the *New Cambridge Modern History, volume nine*.

Documentary material

Documentary materials are scattered. Apart from the Sauvigny work mentioned above the following are recommended: *Metternich's Europe 1813–1848*, edited by Mack Walker and published by Harper Torchbooks, 1968. Also *Documents in the Political History of the European Continent 1815–1939*, edited by G. A. Kertesz and published by Oxford University Press, 1968. No serious student of Metternich should fail to read the 'Political Testament' that he addressed to Alexander in 1820. This is to be found in *Metternich's Europe*, pp. 112–27.

For a broad understanding of the period D. Thomson's *Europe since Napoleon* (Longmans, 1957, re-issued in Pelican, 1966) is invaluable – mainly parts two and three.

Other specialist works of particular relevance are:

E. WANGERMANN, *From Joseph II to the Jacobin Trials* (Oxford University Press, 1959), a useful commentary on the nature of the regime inherited by Metternich.

R. W. SETON-WATSON, *A History of the Czechs and Slovaks* (1943: re-issued by Archon, 1965).

G. BARANY, *Széchenyi and the Awakening of Hungarian Nationalism* (Oxford University Press, 1969).

P. VIERECK, *Conservatism Revisited* (first published 1949 and re-issued, with additions, by Collier Books, 1962).

Index

INDEX 187